CLIMB THE HILL WITH JESUS

Lent

Scriptural Readings & Reflections

Ash Wednesday to Wednesday of Holy Week

Revised and Expanded

Cycles:
A –2008
B–2009
C–2010

Alonso de Blas, O.F.M.

Tau-publishing

Book layout and design: Arlene F. Besore
Cover Art: Francesca Bianco

The poetic structure of passages written in verse (for example,
Psalms, Wisdom, Isaiah, etc.) have been preserved in verse as printed
by inserting / marks.

For re-orders and other publications as well as our daily updated
web site with Scriptural Reflections and meditations visit us at

Tau-publishing.com

ISBN: 978-0-9796766-6-6
Printed in U.S.A.
Second edition: December 2007
© 2007 by Tau publishing

GENERAL INTRODUCTION

The word Lent comes from Lenten, the Middle English word for spring-time, so it is a natural for calling attention to the preparations that lead up to the flowering of spring, a return from the darkness and gloom of winter to the blooming of spring with new life, new hopes, a season of renewal for the whole world (if you happen to live in the northern hemisphere, that is). In its religious use, it is related to the celebration of Easter, the great and holy beginning of our New and Risen Life in Christ.

For the first few centuries, the church prepared for Easter by fasting for only two or three days, then by fasting the entire week preceding Easter (what would become our "Holy Week"). But as early as the fourth century it had developed into the Lent of forty days that we've grown up with. It's clear that when Christianity was made kosher by the conversion of Constantine, the Roman Emperor and son of St. Helen, there was a wave of newly-interested candidates for entry into this intriguing and suddenly safe "in" religion.

This forty-day period allowed interested parties to show their good will by making a break with their past lives, and allowed the churches to make a careful presentation of our faith, thus making possible a mutual examination and judgment of and by the catechumen (the name for our candidates for Baptism-Confirmation-Eucharist) and the church they sought to enter. Parishes that use the RCIA (the Rite of Christian Initiation of Adults) get to witness and enjoy the process of mutual examination and prayerful encouragement that culminates in the Initiation of their new brothers and sisters at the Holy Saturday night services.

The spirit of Lent is expressed in the traditional three prongs of prayer, self-denial, and almsgiving. We are asked to intensify our awareness of the need for more room for God in our lives by embarking on a regimen of increased prayer, spiritual reading, quiet time for reflection, making the Stations of the Cross especially on the Fridays of Lent, etc.

We discipline ourselves by the ancient practices of fasting (only one full meal a day) and abstaining from meat (a luxury in days of yore), specifically on Ash Wednesday and Good Friday, but also on the Fridays of Lent. The perennial "what are you giving up for Lent?" points to the purifying value of an ancient ascetical practice. These days we like to remind Catholics how beneficial it would be to also ask "what are you taking on for Lent?" because the acquisition of increased virtue (visiting the sick, reading for the blind, serving meals at kitchens for the homeless, etc.) would not come to an end with Easter (as would the temporary ban on chocolate, for example) but would lead to yearly growth, like rings around a tree trunk.

And the giving of alms is another powerful and practical way to cut back on attention to ourselves so as to be ready to give more attention to others—the money you save on movie tickets for your enjoyment you can spend for children's books/toys at a shelter for mothers seeking safety for their families.

Liturgically, Lent begins on Ash Wednesday and ends six weeks later after Wednesday of Holy Week, issuing in the Triduum, the high point of the entire liturgical year, with its subsequent cooling-down period of fifty days that ends at Pentecost with the coming of the promised Holy

Spirit into the gathered community of Jesus' followers. <u>Barren Earth To New Growth</u>, the companion volume to this Lenten booklet (available from Tau publishing), serves as your guide through the Triduum.

[A note to the reader:
In this booklet we will present a guide to the Scriptural readings for every Mass, to provide the framework for the reflections presented. Some times in a condensed form of the Scripture passage (with quotes in italics), at other times paraphrased into a synopsis. In neither case do we mean to replace the reading of the entire text of God's word, always cited and readily available, and proclaimed by the lector and presider at each Mass.]

Ash Wednesday

Introduction

Ever since the times of Old Testament calls for repentance and for changing over from a sinful life to a clean new start, the wearing of (sackcloth and) ashes was the public sign of putting an end to a mistaken way of life so as to begin anew, after a period of purification, in a clean new direction. We find the same notion in what we naively call "primitive" religions in their sophisticated use of "renewable resources" to demonstrate the process of putting an end to the old and then making a new beginning: cutting off hair and fingernails. (A quicker, more dramatic demonstration involved cleansing by ritual stripping and bathing or jumping repeatedly through fire.)

Scripture

Joel 2:12-18 *Return to me with your whole heart, with fasting, and weeping, and mourning; rend your hearts, not your garments, and return to the Lord, your God. For gracious and merciful is he, slow to anger, rich in kindness, and relenting in punishment.*

Responsorial Psalm 51: 3-4, 5-6, 12-13, 14, 17

2 Corinthians 5:20 - 6:2 *Be reconciled to God! For our sakes God made him who did not know sin to be sin, so that in him we might become the very holiness of God. Now is the acceptable time!*

Matthew 6:1-6, 16-18 *Be on guard against performing religious acts for people to see. Otherwise expect no recompense from your heavenly Father.*

Reflection:

Around five hundred years before Christ, Joel warns the people to prepare for judgment on the coming Day of the Lord by repenting—but not just outwardly: *"rend your hearts, not your garments!"* (In Romans 2:28 Paul will note that true circumcision is not outward, in the flesh but rather, *"of the heart, in the spirit."* And already in the fifth book of the Bible we hear the command *"Circumcise your hearts"* Deuteronomy 10:16.)

In the Gospel Jesus warns against making an outward show of our repentance in the traditional trio of helping others, praying and fasting. If what you do is for people's applause, that's what you'll get, but don't expect your Father's blessing, because you weren't really doing it for him. Personally, I've always found it a bit disconcerting to read (on this day of all days!) "When you fast, see to it that you groom your hair and wash your face. In that way no one can see you are fasting but your Father and [he] will repay you." I guess that shows just how human we are—we can still use the external reminder. (By the way, in an inspired bit of spiritual recycling we get our ashes for today from the burning of the palms left over from last year's Palm Sunday. Full circle.) Paul pleads with us to not miss the chance the Father gives us when he sends his son so close to us, since "for our sakes God made him who did not know sin to be sin, so that in him we might become the very holiness of God" (emphases added). So close to us in our sinfulness that you might say we rubbed off on him, but miraculously, he rubbed off on us! As Jesus leaves behind his divinity to put on our frail humanity, we are by the same token able, and in fact called, to leave behind our sinful humanity and put on the very holiness of God.

Thursday after Ash Wednesday

Scripture

Deuteronomy 30: 15-20 *Moses said to the people: "Today I have set before you life and prosperity, death and doom. If you obey the Lord your God, loving him and walking in his ways, and keeping his commandments, the Lord your God will bless you."*

Responsorial Psalm 1: 1-2, 3, 4, 6

Luke 9: 22-25 *Jesus said to all: "Whoever loses his life for my sake will save it. What profit does he show who gains the whole world and destroys himself in the process?"*

Reflection:
One thing about taking stock of your life, where is it headed, what does it mean…it forces you to get your priorities straight. The church, like a good mother watching her child getting ready to leave home and set out into life, clearly wants a showdown, an either/or. Either you're going to

waste your time going after "good times" and fun, or you're going to get down to brass tacks and use your time and energy building up a life. The latter will take planning and sacrifice but will yield solid results. The former takes no thought, little effort, but fritters away your opportunities until reality—usually with a thud!—sets in and demands you clean up your act.

Guess what? It's that time. STOP. Consider where you are, as opposed to where God wants you to be. In terms of the American Dream: what good was it to get more toys but have no time to play with them? What did you gain by getting that promotion but losing your wife and kids because you were never around them since you were giving 110% at the office? So now you have this great big beautiful house but you both have to work to make the payments, so you don't have much time to spend in it. You finally made it into the "in" crowd but you lost the friends that made your life a joy…I could go on….

Today is step one. Make your choice—and live it. Choose to make more room for God in your life by moving yourself out of the center and letting God show you his priorities. They won't be hard to find…he wants you to be as loving as you can be with the love he's given you. You have it in you—let it out! You want targets? Look around…see anybody in need of something you have? Share it. Give some of your self away. It's the only way you'll grow into your best self. You want to save your life for yourself? You'll lose it. Or weren't you listening to the Gospel today?

Friday after Ash Wednesday

Scripture

Isaiah 58:1-9 God tells Isaiah to remind the people of their wickedness: They ask me why I don't seem to notice their fasting, but they fill their fast day with their own pursuits, and end up quarreling with their workers.

You think lying in sackcloth and ashes will do it? *"This, rather, is the fasting that I wish, sharing your bread with the hungry, sheltering the oppressed and the homeless, clothing the naked, and not turning your back on your own." Then, when they call, I will answer them.*

Responsorial Psalm 51: 3-4, 5-6, 18-19

Matthew 9: 14-15 *When the day comes that the groom is taken away, then you will fast.*

Reflection:
Fasting is one of the hallmarks of this penitential season. Why? It reminds us of the plight of the poor, who go hungry as a way of life. What must it be like to feel not only the pangs of your own hunger, but the pain of watching your children or others who count on you go hungry too? There's little merit in just suffering (remember G. Gordon Liddy holding his hand over a flame until the flesh burned?), but if we withhold something from our own use so that we can have it to share with others who need it, we're on track.

True fasting is not just the external going without food. It is an internal discipline as well, that leads to insight into the proper amount/place/ importance of our material goods rather than just their thoughtless (and/ or conspicuous) consumption. Doesn't it just kill you to read about what sometimes happens after a natural disaster in some faraway place, that planeloads of food are not able to reach the victims of the disaster because the distribution trucks have been commandeered by local big shots who then steal and/or try to sell the donated goods? Go ahead, feel the righteous indignation…. Now—think how <u>God</u> must feel when he put the earth into our hands and asked us to have dominion over it IN HIS NAME, and now has to watch us mess up the proper distribution of HIS GOODS, goods that we "own" because he has DONATED them to us? Just a thought.

I guess you would expect a Franciscan to go nutso on poverty, material goods, and the like. But I do consider it off-balance to go for poverty for its own sake (Gordon Liddy again). I don't think God is happy to see any of his children lacking what they need. But if poverty per se is not virtuous, then consider the virtue of detachment: if you don't need it and don't have it, don't sweat it. If you have it and don't need it, enjoy it but be ready to share with someone else who might need it. And if more people shared this attitude, there might not be so much need that we just shrug it off. If you can't do anything about the global situation, look at the local one: supply or assist or serve food at kitchens for the poor, don't just applaud the efforts of St. Vincent de Paul volunteers— take their place once in a while, help set up/maintain shelters for children or single mothers, tutor a student struggling at school, etc. etc. Give of your SELF, after all, it was a gift from God to you.

Saturday after Ash Wednesday

Scripture

Isaiah 58: 9-14 *If you bestow your bread on the hungry and satisfy the afflicted then the Lord will guide you always. / He will renew your strength, and you shall be like a spring whose water never fails. / If you honor the Lord's holy day by not following your ways [or] seeking your own interests, then you shall delight in the Lord.*

Responsorial Psalm 86: 1-2, 3-4, 5-6

Luke 5: 27-32 *The Pharisees and scribes said to his disciples, "Why do you eat and drink with tax collectors and non-observers of the law?" Jesus said to them, "The healthy do not need a doctor, sick people do. I have not come to invite the self-righteous to a change of heart, but sinners."*

Reflection:

God is not satisfied by the externals of religion, but by sincere observance of the requirements of religion: helping others from your heart as well as your wallet, a true respect for the Lord's day, using it not to further your own agenda, but God's. Just attending Sunday Mass does not cut it—you must live its message once you leave the confines of the church building. You do that, and you become a walking, talking Mass for the ones who weren't inside with you; you pass on to them the goodness of God that filled you when you attended the Eucharist, making you "a spring whose water never fails."

From Luke, evangelist and physician, we understand that the only people whom a doctor has no way of healing are those who don't seek his help. Here we see Jesus the healer going out to make house calls, accepting invitations to eat with those that no good Pharisee would be caught dead sharing a meal with, reaching out to invite them to the banquet of life that only his Father seems willing to call them to.

Lucky for us Jesus is not disgusted by sinners, but is eager to draw us out of sin and into awareness of our status as once dead-in-sin but now alive-in-the-Spirit. All we have to do is listen to his call to repent, rely on his strength and grace, and make that change of heart, that metanoia which wipes out the old and makes room for the new. Not because we deserve it or have earned it, but because of God's merciful love. Let's not waste this chance. Let's answer the call. Today.

First Sunday of Lent

Cycle A – Scripture:

Genesis 2:7-9; 3: 1-7 The Lord made man, planted a garden, and placed the tree of life and the tree of knowledge of good and evil in the middle of the garden. The serpent tricked the woman into eating the fruit, and she gave some to her husband. *Then the eyes of both were opened, and they realized they were naked; so they sewed fig leaves together and made loincloths for themselves.*

Responsorial Psalm 51: 3-4, 5-6, 12-13, 14, 17

Romans 5: 12-19 (shorter 5:12, 17-19) *Just as a single offense brought condemnation to all men, a single righteous act brought all men acquittal and life. Just as through one man's disobedience all became sinners, so through one man's obedience all shall become just.*

Matthew 4: 1-11 Led into the desert by the Spirit to be tempted by the devil, Jesus fasted forty days and forty nights, and was hungry. The devil suggested he turn the stones (round, loaf-shaped) into bread, but Jesus quotes Scripture: "Not by bread alone is man to live…." So the devil takes him to the temple tower and quotes some Scripture himself: "He will bid his angels take care of you, that you may never stumble on a stone;" and dares him to take the plunge. Jesus answers: Scripture also has it: "You shall not put the Lord your God to the test." Finally, the devil offers him all the kingdoms of the world if only he prostrates himself in homage to him. Jesus counters angrily: Away with you, Satan! Scripture says "You shall do homage to the Lord your God; him alone shall you adore."

Reflection:

From Genesis we revisit the historical entry of sin into our world, the original sin that polluted the stream right from its source. It's pride, pure and simple. We disobey because we do not like being limited. The list of sins will escalate and their depravity will plummet, till we find our lives stunted. But Paul announces the undoing of all this by the proper response, the obedience, of one man, the New Adam, who makes possible a new start for a rescued mankind. And Matthew presents this one obedient man as the New Israel of God, undoing the forty years of wandering and rebellion in the desert by his forty days and nights of obedient following of God's plan for him in the Scriptures, culminating in his successful showdown with the devil.

First Sunday of Lent

Cycle B – Scripture

Genesis 9: 6-15 *God said to Noah and his sons with him, "See, I am now establishing my covenant with you and with every living creature that was with you. There shall not be another flood to devastate the earth. I set my bow in the clouds to serve as a sign of the covenant between me and the earth, so that the waters shall never again become a flood to destroy all mortal beings.*

Responsorial Psalm 25: 4-5, 6-7, 8-9

1 Peter 3:18-22 *[In] Noah's day, a few persons escaped in the ark through the water. You are now saved by a baptismal bath which corresponds to this exactly.*

Mark 1: 12-15 *The Spirit sent Jesus out toward the desert. He stayed in the wasteland forty days, put to the test there by Satan. After John's arrest, he [proclaimed]: "This is the time of fulfillment! The reign of God is at hand! Reform your lives and believe in the Good News."*

Reflection:

Our God is such a lousy negotiator: when we goof up one covenant he figures, OK, that didn't work, let's try a different one. He won't hold our feet to the fire; he's too interested in getting our feet moving in the right direction. So now there is a covenant with Noah and the survivors of the flood. Don't you just love the reason for the rainbow in the clouds? It's not for poets or artists—it's to remind himself to turn off the water this time!

Peter's selection is included because it portrays the <u>other</u> face of water: sinners are swallowed up in the waters of death, e.g. the Egyptians in their chariots, and in this case, all the others who were not aboard the ark. In this picture, baptism is our entry into God's saving ark that keeps us safe from the waters of death and sin. The water symbol is powerful: unrepentant sinners drown in the waters of sin, but repentant sinners enter the waters to die with Christ so as to rise with him to new life!

As usual with Mark, the telling takes few words. The Spirit leads Jesus to the desert to prepare himself for his mission. He was tempted by the devil (no word on the process, but we know the outcome). As soon as his precursor exits the scene, Jesus begins his campaign for the reign of God: The time is now! Believe it and reform your lives! Here again we see our God's concern for our salvation. We are given one last call so we can put our past behind us (by God's gracious love), clean up our act, and this time really do a good job of following him home to the Father.

First Sunday of Lent

Cycle C – Scripture

Deuteronomy 26: 4-10 *Moses told the people, "You shall declare before the Lord your God: 'My father was a wandering Aramean who went down to Egypt as an alien.'"* The Hebrews prospered and grew in numbers. When the Egyptians turned on them, and began to persecute them, they cried to the Lord, the God of their fathers, and he heard their cry. *"The Lord brought us out of Egypt with his outstretched arm and he gave us this land flowing with milk and honey."* Moses has them bring the first fruits of their harvest in this new land, and offer them to God in recognition of his generosity with them. And after they make this offering, *"then you and your family and the aliens who live among you shall make merry over all these good things which the Lord, your God, has given you."*

Responsorial Psalm 91: 1-2, 10-11, 12-13, 14-15

Romans 10: 8-13 *If you confess with your lips that Jesus is Lord, and believe in your heart that God raised him from the dead, you will be saved. Here there is no difference between Jew and Greek; all have the same Lord, rich in mercy toward all who call upon him. Everyone who calls on the name of the Lord will be saved.*

Luke 4: 1-13 *Jesus was led by the Spirit into the desert for forty days, where he was tempted by the devil, "Command this stone to turn into bread; prostrate yourself before me and it shall all be yours; throw yourself down from here." When the devil had finished all this tempting he left him, to await another opportunity.*

Reflection:
What a beautiful scene, for Americans so reminiscent of that first Thanksgiving at our first harvest in our new land. What a pointed reminder of the Israelites' roots as one-time aliens, and their total dependence on God, so that, as they give God the credit for their success, they share it with the (fellow) aliens living among them! Hmm…think of the Thanksgivings being celebrated along the southwestern borders of our own country….

If we would believe in our hearts what comes so easily to our lips, we would be living, and not just referring to, our faith in this merciful God who makes no distinctions—Jew vs. Greek (Gentile) is as black-and-white a disjunctive as they knew. And yet, in Christ we have all been saved. Does any of that "God loves us and not them" remain in our minds or hearts or behaviors? How can it, if our hearts mean what our lips say?

Jesus re-lives the life of the whole Jewish people. In his forty days in the desert he replays (and this time, gets it right!) the forty years of wanderings and temptation of the Old Testament experience of his people. But it ends on an ominous note—can you hear the movie score turning dark?—"the devil…left him, to await another opportunity." Good old Jesus: he keeps on trying to teach us the right way, giving us not only his example, but his strength…if only we believed in our hearts what we say with our lips….

Monday First Week

Scripture

Leviticus 19: 1-2, 11-18 *Be holy, for I, the Lord, your God, am holy. You shall not steal [nor] lie or speak falsely to one another. / You shall not defraud your neighbor. / Show neither partiality to the weak nor deference to the mighty, but judge your fellow men justly. / You shall not bear hatred for your brother in your heart. / You shall love your neighbor as yourself. I am the Lord.*

Responsorial Psalm 19: 8, 9, 10, 15

Matthew 25: 31-46 Jesus' description of the Last Judgment is stark, and full of surprises. When he returns in glory, the Son of Man will separate the good guys from the bad guys and judge each group—on the basis, not of their church attendance, nor how well they have memorized their prayers, but how they have dealt with the needy! What a revelation: turns out that every time they were kind to some poor yokel, they were actually tending to Jesus! Of course, the revelation in reverse is a real bummer! Can you see their faces when they ask—whaddayamean? We never passed <u>you</u> by; we'd never do that to <u>you</u>, Lord. Ouch.

Reflection:
After the first three commandments of the law point out our primary obligations towards God, the next seven deal with our behavior towards one another. Our godly life must be a holy life. In all our dealings with one another we are to show justice and love, as God does to us. (In keeping with the rudimentary nature of these commandments, I love the specific prohibitions against the infantile, guilty pleasures of cursing the deaf or putting stumbling blocks in the way of the blind.) And talk about social justice issues (nothing infantile here): "you shall not withhold overnight the wages of your day laborer." What is it they say—justice delayed is justice denied? Proper behavior is a challenge: "Be holy as I am holy."

And, as usual, Jesus' teaching asks us to go beyond the minimal legal requirements of the code that was used to "break us in" to proper behavior back in the Old Testament days. There's no law that requires us to meet every need; we aren't breaking any commandments if we go about our business without taking notice of people around us. But it sure doesn't mesh with Jesus and his coming kingdom!

I've often thought how immensely helpful this message of Jesus is for anyone interested in following him. No esoteric requirements that only a few can meet, no lists of rules and regulations that must be memorized, just a vivid and ever-so practical guide to everyday living. It may be simple, but it's not easy—it's a challenge: "Be holy as I am holy."

Tuesday First Week

Scripture

Isaiah 55: 10-11 *My word that goes forth from my mouth shall not return to me void, but shall do my will, achieving the end for which I sent it.*

Responsorial Psalm 34: 4-5, 6-7, 16-17, 18-19

Matthew 6: 7-15 *Your Father knows what you need before you ask him. If you forgive the faults of others, your heavenly Father will forgive you yours. If you do not, neither will your Father forgive you.*

Reflection:

What a powerful image: as God sends down his rain to water the earth and make it fertile, so does he send his word, through the prophets, with every intention of having it penetrate our hard hearts and make them yield for him a harvest of goodness. It would take quite an obstinate heart to remain hard and unyielding before such a loving, gently persistent God. Let's not make it difficult for God. Let's not make him sorry he gave us a free will, so he could invite a meaningful, free correspondence from us, instead of just forcing the proper (but, alas, meaningless) response from us.

Isn't it wonderful that we don't have to worry about God not understanding our requests? He already knows what we need—even before we ask him. But we'd better be careful when we ask: how can we expect to receive his forgiveness for having offended him, if we are unwilling to offer ours to those who've offended us?

Wednesday First Week

Scripture

Jonah 3: 1-10 The Assyrians are the mighty enemies of the Israelites, and Nineveh is their capital city. Asking Jonah to go there to preach repentance and submission to his God is like asking a televangelist to go to Taliban country and tell them they must submit, not to Allah, but to God the Father. This is why it took two tries (the ship going in the opposite direction, the frightening storms…it's a whale of a story!) to get Jonah to go. Jonah belatedly but bravely begins his preaching tour, and, stop the press! Everyone accepts his message, "the people proclaimed a fast and put on sackcloth," all the way up to the king! So God spares them. (The end of the story is not included, but it's too good to miss: turns out Jonah is not happy with the results! He'd been hoping to see Yahweh's wrath blaze down on these traditional enemies of his people. Lesson: they may look like enemies to us, but God has no enemies, only children.)

Responsorial Psalm 51: 3-4, 12-13, 18-19

Luke 11: 29-32 *Just as Jonah was a sign for the Ninevites, so will the Son of Man be for the present age. At the judgment, the citizens of Nineveh will rise along with the present generation, and they will condemn it. For at the preaching of Jonah they reformed, but you have a greater than Jonah here.*

Reflection:

The story of Jonah has a dramatic beginning, a dramatic middle, and a dramatic end. We are at the middle, when, less than halfway into his preaching mission, Jonah finds that the preaching task he had accepted so reluctantly and fearfully has been enthusiastically accepted by the very enemies of God's people! Jesus rebukes his audience for their hardness of heart and their unwillingness to accept his message. "So you won't believe me unless I show you a sign? I'll show you a sign, all right, but not what you expect...some cheap trick, something to wow you. You'll have to settle for the sign of Jonah...." The prophet's three days in the belly of the whale will be replayed in Jesus' three days in his tomb. "Let's see if you believe that! Your fathers believed the words of a prophet, but you're witnessing greater words, and greater works, than those of any prophet...yet you still refuse to believe."

What a break for us that we can so easily find our way to the sacrament of Reconciliation. We hear the call to reform; we receive the courage to take stock and make changes; we find the forgiveness of Jesus close at hand. And we don't have to earn any of this, but only to come to appreciate the efforts Jesus makes to reach out to us—even in our sin.

Thursday First Week

Scripture

Esther Chapter C (follows ch. 4): **12, 14-16, 23-25** *Queen Esther prayed to the God of Israel, "Help me, who am alone and have no help but you. As a child I [heard] that you chose Israel from among all peoples, and that you fulfilled all your promises to them. Save us by your power and help me, who am alone and have no one but you, O Lord."*

Responsorial Psalm 138: 1-2, 2-3, 7-8

Matthew 7: 7-12 *Ask, and you will receive. Would one of you hand his son a stone when he asks for a loaf? If you, with all your sins, know how to give your children what is good, how much more will your heavenly Father give good things to anyone who asks him?*

Reflection:

The first reading is quite dramatic. Queen Esther, the Jewish wife of the Persian king, must defend herself and her people against a plot by Haman, her jealous and conniving adversary, who was convincing the king that no Jew could be loyal to him, because of their unique religious beliefs. Esther appeals to the God of her people, who has so often and powerfully saved them in past crises, in words that ache with helplessness and need: "help me, who am alone and have no one but you, O Lord."

Jesus argues that since even a human father never fails to do his best to meet his trusting child's request, we can be sure that our heavenly Father will never fail to give us, not only good things, but what's best for us. All we have to do is call upon him, he'll be there with the answer to our problems.

Unfortunately, the problem (to paraphrase Pogo) is us. We find it so difficult to be a trusting child, after so many years of looking after ourselves, thank you very much. As long as we rely on ourselves to provide solutions, we cannot truly call upon our Father as helpless, trusting children ("I am alone, and have no one but you"), so we are getting in the way of our own rescue. As long as we're "secretly" counting on ourselves, we're not allowing God to be the saving Father he can, and wants to, be.

Friday First Week

Scripture

Ezekiel 18: 21-28 *Do I derive any pleasure from the death of the wicked? says the Lord God. Do I not rather rejoice when he turns from his evil way that he may live? If a wicked man, turning from the wickedness he has committed, does what is right and just, he shall preserve his life.*

Responsorial Psalm 130: 1-2, 3-4, 5-6, 7-8

Matthew 5:20-26 Jesus warns his disciples that their holiness must surpass that of the professionally holy people (scribes and Pharisees). Observance of the law is like the "Minimum Daily Requirement," it's just enough for them to maintain, but not enough to grow. The law against murder doesn't go far enough, it actually forbids you to hate or revile or hold your neighbor in contempt. Then there's that challenging: *"If you bring your gift to the altar and there recall that your brother has anything against you, leave your gift at the altar, go first to be reconciled with your brother, and then come and offer your gift."* How can you think you'll reconcile with your Father in heaven if you don't first reconcile with your brother right in front of you?

Reflection:
You could call this the "Mass of Reconciliation." In Ezekiel God clears away any remnant of the old "clan" thinking, making each person responsible for his own behavior. If a good man chooses evil, that choice is responsible for his death. But if an evil man repents his behavior and returns to good, he will save his life. Each person is called to loyalty to God. And, if you've been disloyal in the past, reconciliation is what God desires, offers, and encourages.

And please notice where Jesus puts the emphasis in his gift-at-the-altar scene. It's not: if you have anything against your brother, go straighten it (him) out; it's: if he's got anything against you—hold everything! You know what that means? It means that even if you're pretty darned sure it's not your fault, but he still somehow remains convinced it is, you've got to sit down and address the issue, rather than blithely passing it off as his mistake and getting on with your life. Good luck to us all!

Saturday First Week

Scripture

Deuteronomy 26: 16-19 *Provided you keep all his commandments, you will be a people sacred to the Lord, your God, as he promised. Today you are making this agreement with the Lord.*

Responsorial Psalm 119: 1-2, 4-5, 7-8

Matthew 5:43-48 *You have heard the commandment, "You shall love your countryman but hate your enemy." My command to you is: love your enemies, pray for your persecutors. This will prove that you are sons of your heavenly Father, for his sun rises on the bad and the good, the just and the unjust. If you love those who love you, what merit is there in that? You must be made perfect as your heavenly Father is perfect.*

Reflection:

Today is the day to recall and renew our covenant with God— or, more correctly, his covenant with us. Because it's basically unfair; it's really unilateral. He gains nothing from us but the loyalty he's already entitled to as our Creator. (Actually, it's our love he's really after.) We rise in stature from one among many to "the one." We are his choice; he stretches out his hand to take ours—something we could never manage on our initiative. You just stick with me, and I'll share everything I have with you. What a God!

The beauty of this covenant is that his magnanimity rubs off on us. Ideally, we begin to act unilaterally to others, as he does to us. Today's gospel challenges us to go beyond what is just (human expectation), to what is loving (Godly behavior). It's no great shakes to be nice to somebody who's nice to you. Try doing a favor for somebody who always turns you down when you ask him for a favor. Now think of God dealing with us all our lives, and the lives of all humanity down through the ages. Will he never learn? Wait, we're the ones supposed to learn...to stop holding people to their word, to stretch ourselves beyond justice to forgiveness, to not loving prudently (just the ones who are sure to love us back) but foolishly, lavishly, in the perfect way of our Father.

Second Sunday of Lent

Cycle A – Scripture

Genesis 12: 1-4 *The Lord said to Abram: "Go forth from the land of your father's house to a land that I will show you. I will make of you a great nation, and I will bless you. All the communities of the earth shall find blessing in you."*

Responsorial Psalm 33: 4-5, 18-19, 20, 22

2 Timothy 1: 8-10 *God has saved us and has called us to a holy life, not because of any merit of ours but according to his own design—the grace held out to us in Christ Jesus.*

Matthew 17: 1-9 *Jesus took Peter, James, and his brother John and led them up on a high mountain. He was transfigured before their eyes. His face became as dazzling as the sun, his clothes as radiant as light. Suddenly a bright cloud overshadowed them, [and] a voice said, "This is my beloved Son on whom my favor rests. Listen to him." As they were coming down the mountain Jesus commanded them, "Do not tell anyone of the vision until the Son of Man rises from the dead."*

Reflection:

There's a steady stream of good news this Sunday, but it ends on an ominous note. From Genesis we see Yahweh's favor extended to Abram, and happily so, because the man so obviously trusts in God's call that he leaves behind all his security systems (the work of a lifetime, really) to follow the Lord's plan for him. We should all be this detachable from our plans and give way to God's designs for our lives, even when no maps are supplied, just a voice saying, "Leave all your accomplishments behind and follow me—we'll start all over again somewhere else." Paul reaffirms God's gracious call to holiness, based not on any merit of ours, but solely on his outreaching love for us, with Jesus as his point man.

Then we come to today's highlight: his intimates are invited to a special event—they will see Jesus endowed with the dazzling glory that is his due. They thrill at the sight of Jesus conversing with Moses and Elijah (the personification of the law and the prophets—the two sources of all their revelation). And they are overcome as they hear the voice of God coming out of a shining cloud, bestowing his official approval on Jesus, their Jesus, their teacher and friend. But there's that jarring final note: it seems all this has happened so as to bolster their faith against the day of Jesus' death….

Second Sunday of Lent

Cycle B – Scripture

Genesis 22: 1-2, 9, 10-13, 15-18 God tests Abraham, to see how genuine is his faith. He asks him to offer his precious Isaac, the supposed source of the myriads of descendants he was promised, as a holocaust in his honor. When father and son arrive at the place designated by God, Abraham painfully but obediently prepares to slaughter his boy, building an altar, stacking on the wood, and now, knife in hand, ready to do the unthinkable. God is duly impressed and stops the action, providing a ram caught in a nearby thicket to serve as the sacrifice. *"I swear by myself, says the Lord, that because you acted as you did in not withholding from me your beloved son, I will bless you abundantly and make your descendants as countless as the stars of the sky and the sands of the seashore; and in your descendants all the nations of the earth shall find blessing—all this because you obeyed my command."*

23

Responsorial Psalm 116: 10, 15, 16-17, 18-19

Romans 8: 31-34 *If God is for us, who can be against us? Is it possible that he who did not spare his own Son but handed him over for the sake of us all will not grant us all things besides? Who will condemn? Christ Jesus, who died [and] was raised up and intercedes for us?*

Mark 9: 2-10 *Jesus took Peter, James and John off by themselves with him and led them up a high mountain. He was transfigured before their eyes and his clothes became dazzlingly white. Elijah and Moses were in conversation with Jesus. Peter spoke [but] he hardly knew what to say, for they were all overcome with awe. A cloud overshadowed them, and a voice [said]: "This is my Son, my beloved. Listen to him." As they were coming down the mountain, he [forbade] them to tell anyone what they had seen before the Son of Man had risen from the dead. They kept this word to themselves, though they continued to discuss what "to rise from the dead" meant.*

Reflection:
The first two readings play off each other wonderfully. In the first God can only go so far in his testing of Abraham's faith before he stops everything and owns up to the fact that he was only testing him, he would never ask such a thing from Abraham, but is greatly impressed by Abraham's willingness, which suffices to garner great blessings in return. This all makes it even more impressive when we read in Paul that God did not spare his <u>own</u> Son, but handed him over for the sake of us all. Why doesn't <u>God's</u> willingness suffice? My guess is that God sent his Son to do whatever it took to convince us of the greatness of his fatherly love for us. And that's what Jesus chose to do—whatever it took, emptying himself of his former glory, taking on our lowly human estate, taking on all our weaknesses, even death—death on a cross (Philippians 2: 6ff). And the Father can only look on in pain, hoping the lesson will not be lost on us.

At his Transfiguration, Jesus will give his intimates a glimpse of that former glory that he chose to lay aside when he came as one of us in all things but sin. They are duly wowed. Peter hardly knows what he's saying, he just wants to prolong the vision. But soon it ends, and they see "only Jesus," their teacher and friend, who enjoins them from discussing any of this until the Son of Man rises from the dead. They keep wondering what "to rise from the dead" meant! Pobrecitos, they have no idea, in spite of his explicit warnings, that first he must suffer and die before he regains his glory as God's Son. And that they must follow that exact path, each carrying his own cross, so as to enter with him into the Father's glory.

Second Sunday of Lent

Cycle C – Scripture

Genesis 15: 5-12, 17-18 God took Abram outside and said: *"Look up at the sky and count the stars, if you can. Just so shall your descendants be."* Yahweh offers Abram a descendance as numerous as the stars in the sky, the sands on the shore. Abram puts his faith in the Lord, who credits it to him as an act of righteousness and loyalty—especially considering the odds. When Abram asks for a pledge, God orders: *"Bring me a three-year-old heifer, a three-year-old she-goat, a three-year-old ram, a turtledove, and a young pigeon."* He had Abram split them in two and place the halves opposite each other, the customary arrangement of a covenant sacrifice. Abram fell into a trance, *"and there appeared a smoking brazier and a flaming torch which passed between those pieces. [Then] the Lord made a covenant with Abram, saying: 'To your descendants I give this land.'"*

Responsorial Psalm 27: 1, 7-8, 8-9, 13-14

Philippians 3: 17 – 4: 1 *Be imitators of me. Take as your guide those who follow the example that we set. We have our citizenship in heaven; it is from there that we eagerly await the coming of our savior, the Lord Jesus Christ. Continue to stand firm in the Lord.*

Luke 9: 28-36 *Jesus took Peter, John and James and went up onto a mountain to pray. While he was praying, his face changed in appearance and his clothes became dazzlingly white. Suddenly two men were talking with him—Moses and Elijah. Peter and those with him saw his glory and likewise saw the two men standing with him. A cloud came and overshadowed them. Then from the cloud came a voice which said, "This is my Son, my Chosen One. Listen to him."*

Reflection:

In the Semitic culture, a covenant was a formal agreement between two parties, who passed between the two halves of split animals, signifying the fate that they called upon themselves if they were disloyal to their mutual agreement. Here the torch symbolizes God. Notice how the initiative, and all the action, is God's: he calls for the covenant; he passes through the split halves; he promises countless descendants. Later, he will give the commandments which his people will follow as their part in this agreement.

Paul urges the Christians at Philippi to stand firm in the Lord, and continue to follow the example of those who live no longer for this world, but recognize that they belong to heaven (God) and live accordingly, faithful to their New Covenant.

Remember Jesus at the last supper, asking them to drink from the cup of the "new and everlasting covenant?" The next day his body will be not quite split, but broken and drained of its blood.

At the Transfiguration the disciples receive a glimpse, a sneak preview, of the glory which belongs to Jesus, acknowledged by the two leading figures of the Law and the Prophets, Moses and Elijah, and presented with the formal approval of heaven's verbal imprimatur. This is the glory of the Risen Christ, who first must undergo a painful and shameful death on the cross, the same road that we must all take: through suffering with Jesus we come to share in the glory of the Risen Christ.

Monday Second Week

Scripture

Daniel 9: 4-10 *Lord, you who keep your merciful covenant toward those who love you and observe your commandments. We have sinned and departed from your commandments. Justice, O Lord, is on your side; we are shamefaced for having sinned against you. But yours, O lord, our God, are compassion and forgiveness!*

Responsorial Psalm 79: 8, 9, 11, 13

Luke 6: 36-38 *Be compassionate, as your Father is compassionate. Do not condemn, and you will not be condemned. Pardon, and you shall be pardoned. For the measure you measure with, will be measured back to you.*

Reflection:
Isn't it wonderful, the confidence that God's dealings with us inspires? Having acknowledged his guilt, Daniel moves directly to claiming God's compassionate pardon. Not because we in any way deserve it. Just because God is clearly so eager to bridge the gap between us that (as I once read somewhere) he is more willing to forgive us than we are to ask him for forgiveness! (And if you don't believe me, remember how Jesus described the loving father of the wayward, prodigal son?) (Hey, maybe that's where I read it!)

The news in the gospel is wonderful, but sobering at the same time. Turns out that God, having given us our free will, is ready to meet us on our level of engagement, whatever that might be. He sets out to accompany us every step of the way, but he has to match our stride to stay with us. If we run, he runs happily with us. If we drag, we force him to drag along too. If we open only a little bit of ourselves to him, then that's all he can pour in of himself—a little bit. The good news is that if we open up a lot, he'll happily fill us a lot. So be careful with the measure you use to reach out to others, because that will set the pace for God's measure of dealing with you. Once again, Jesus is the model. He emptied himself completely (the famous "kenosis" of Philippians 2: 6-11) to make room for the Father's plans, and at his death the Father filled him to the same full extent, so that his body could not remain dead, but was filled with the Holy Sprit and raised again to life.

Tuesday Second Week

Scripture

Isaiah 1: 10, 16-20 *Hear the Lord, princes of Sodom! Listen to God, people of Gomorrah! Cease doing evil; learn to do good. Come now, let us set things right, says the Lord: though your sins be like scarlet, they may become white as snow.*

Responsorial Psalm 50: 8-9, 16-17, 21, 23

Matthew 23: 1-12 *Jesus told the crowds and his disciples: "The scribes and Pharisees have succeeded Moses as teachers; therefore, do everything they tell you. But do not follow their example. Their words are bold but their deeds are few. The greatest among you will be the one who serves the rest."*

Reflection:

Isaiah reveals God's displeasure with his people when he calls them by the names of the ancient wicked cities that went up in smoke. Change your ways: "if you are willing and obey, you shall eat the good things of the land," I will bless you, and not curse you—but you have to stop behaving wickedly. The first step in repenting is to stop, then (re)think, then make the necessary changes to get things right again. How are we doing, already into our second week of this penitential season?

Jesus warns his followers (and the Pharisees themselves!) to not make their practice of religion a pretense, something that only sounds good. Can you imagine the smiles on their faces as they hear Jesus exhort the audience to follow the exhortations of the Pharisees? Can you see those smiles painfully wincing away as the next words come: "Just don't follow their example." Ouch! We shouldn't be "into" religion for ourselves; we should be humbly looking to serve others as our way of serving the Lord.

Wednesday Second Week

Scripture

Jeremiah 18: 18-20 *The men of Judah said, "Let us contrive a plot against Jeremiah. Let us destroy him by his own tongue; let us carefully note his every word." Heed me, O Lord, and remember that I stood before you to speak in their behalf, to turn away your wrath from them.*

Responsorial Psalm 31: 5-6, 14, 15-16

Matthew 20: 17-28 The unnamed, of course (in those times a woman figured only as somebody's wife, or mother, or daughter) mother of Zebedee's sons, comes to Jesus asking him to give her boys the two top places in his kingdom. He answers, *"Sitting at my right hand or my left* *is not mine to give. That is for those for whom it has been reserved by my Father."* You know how the world's great ones make demands on their followers? That's not how it is with me, nor should it be so for any of you, either. If you aspire to greatness you must do so by serving the needs of all. *"The Son of Man has come, not to be served by others, but to serve, to give his life for the many."*

Reflection:
It should not surprise us to learn that in the early Church, the prophet Jeremiah was considered a type (pre-figurement) of Jesus. His career was a constant threat to him, and yet he always answered God's call to take unpopular positions on the events and leaders of his day. And he was persecuted, often and harshly, for his pains. Here we see his reaction to one of the many threats he faced, and kept on facing faithfully, as he lived out his prophetic call. Remind you of anyone?

In today's gospel, Jesus has no sooner finished alerting his little band to the dangers that lie ahead, than along comes a Jewish mother (what can I say…I didn't write the story) asking for special favors for her special (what else?) sons. When the rest of the guys find out what's happened, they flare up at the two brothers (they probably waited until mom was gone). Jesus has to step in and break it up: you want to be the top dog— you've got to serve all the others and not just step to the head of the line and blow the whistle. Look at me. When we look at him at the Last Supper we can hardly believe it. He washes their feet. And then he draws the lesson out for them: You call me Master, and that's what I am. Did you see what I just did? That's what I want you to do. Serve one another. Don't demand service—provide it.

We're coming to halfway of the second week of the season. I wonder how we're doing at coming up with ideas, not just for giving up vices/negatives, but also for taking on virtues/positives. Are there any ways we can be of service to others? Can we try some?

Thursday Second Week

Scripture

Jeremiah 17: 5-10 *Thus says the Lord: Cursed is the man who trusts in human beings, whose heart turns away from the Lord. He is like a barren bush in the desert. Blessed is the man who trusts in the Lord. He is like a tree planted beside the waters.*

Responsorial Psalm 1: 1-2, 3, 4, 6

Luke 16: 19-31 Jesus aims this little story at the Pharisees. *"Once there was a rich man who dressed in purple and linen and feasted splendidly every day."* Makes you wonder if there wasn't more than one well-fed, well-dressed citizen in his audience…. Anyway: there was this poor beggar, Lazarus, all covered with sores, who sat outside his gate, hoping to score some of the scraps off the tablecloths being shaken clean. He dies, and is carried by angels up to the bosom of Abraham—the reward for his patience in suffering. Then the rich man dies, and from the abode of the dead where he was in torment, he looks up to see Abraham and (surprise!) Lazarus resting in his bosom.

You've got to admire the man. He doesn't ask for a pitcher of water, just for Lazarus to dip the tip (what finesse) of his finger in water to refresh his burning tongue, but Abraham reminds him he'd already had his good times, on earth. This is payback time, so Lazarus gets the goodies, and you, golden child, get the shaft. But the man has class. He doesn't complain, but thoughtfully inquires about alerting his five brothers so they won't end up like him. Jesus lays on the irony: *"Abraham answered, 'They have the prophets. Let them hear them.'"* And when the rich man persists, "If someone would only go to them from the dead, then they would repent," Abraham retorts (heavy-duty irony, coming from the mouth of Jesus) *"If they do not listen to Moses and the prophets, they will not be convinced even if one should rise from the dead."* Touché.

Reflection:

You look to this world for strength and for guidance, and you'll end up like a withered, dry bush out in the wastelands. You look to God for guidance and strength, and you'll flourish like a tree planted nice and close to running water, with roots that will always supply for your growth. There is a clear line drawn between the good man and the evil man. So, gentle reader, you'd better make your choice: blessing or curse?

Jesus spins a powerful story for his listeners. He never accuses the rich man of committing a sin: all he does is ignore the needy little beggar. At the end of their lives there is a reversal of fortunes. And recourse to Abraham is fruitless, because he points out the abyss (another line clearly drawn) that separates them, even if they attempted to reach the other. Once again the lesson: put your trust in God, not in this world.

Friday Second Week

Scripture

Genesis 37: 3-4, 12-13, 17-28 *Israel [Jacob] loved Joseph best of all his [twelve] sons.* When his older brothers saw that their father loved him best, they hated him so much that they plotted to kill him. One day, when they saw him coming towards them out in the fields, they said, *"Come, let us kill him and throw him into one of the cisterns here; we could say that a wild beast devoured him."* However, one of them, Reuben, intending to come back and rescue him, said, *"Instead of shedding blood, just throw him into that cistern there in the desert, but don't kill him outright."* When Joseph caught up to them, they threw him into an empty cistern nearby, and then (presumably after saying grace—they weren't pagans, after all) sat down to have their lunch. Looking up, they saw a caravan of Ishmaelites going to Egypt. This time it's Judah who says to his brothers, *"Let us sell him to these Ishmaelites, instead of doing away* *with him ourselves. After all, he is our brother, our own flesh."* So they pulled him up and sold him to them for twenty pieces of silver.

Responsorial Psalm 105: 16-17, 18-19, 20-21
(further details on Joseph as a slave)

Matthew 21: 33-43, 45-46 Jesus addresses this parable to the chief priests and elders of the people. *"There was a property owner who planted a vineyard, put a hedge around it, dug out a vat, and erected a tower. Then he leased it out to tenant farmers and went [away]."* At vintage time he sent for his share of the grapes. The tenants beat one of his slaves and stoned and killed the other two. So he sent more, with the same result. Finally he sent his son, figuring surely he would not receive the same (mis)treatment. But *"when they saw the son, the tenants said, 'Let us kill him and then we shall have his inheritance!'"* So he asks his audience, *"What do you suppose the owner will do to [them]?"* And they answered, *"He will bring that wicked crowd to a bad end and lease his vineyard out to others, who will [deliver his] grapes at vintage time."* So Jesus said to them, "That's why the kingdom of God will be taken away from you and given to others who will yield a rich harvest." When the Pharisees realized he was speaking about them, they tried to arrest him, but they had reason to fear the crowd's reaction.

Reflection:
The patriarch Joseph, the eleventh of Jacob's twelve sons, was a figure of Jesus, resented and persecuted by his own, because his goodness made them so jealous and uncomfortable. Don't you just hurt for the kid, as they plop him away and then sit down to enjoy the lunch that he had just brought them from home? And then that "After all, he is our brother…" as they pocket the twenty pieces of silver (nice work, two apiece).

The figure of God's people as his vineyard is a cliché from Old Testament literature. Yahweh has gone to great lengths: planting, protecting, providing all the care it needs. It's a pretty transparent story of their hard-hearted treatment of his prophets over the centuries, which looks to continue even now, with the arrival of the Son of Man. Jesus sets them up beautifully: you tell me, what's the poor owner supposed to do? And they blithely pronounce their own sentence. What a warning to us on this foreboding Friday, four weeks before Good Friday.

Saturday Second Week

Scripture

Micah 7: 14-15, 16-20 *Who is there like you, the God who removes guilt and pardons sin for the remnant of his inheritance / who does not persist in anger forever, but delights rather in clemency? / You will show faithfulness to Jacob, and grace to Abraham, / as you have sworn to our fathers from days of old.*

Responsorial Psalm 103: 1-2, 3-4, 9-10, 11-12 *Bless the Lord, O my soul, and all my being bless his holy name. / He pardons all your iniquities, he heals all your ills. / He will not always chide, nor does he keep his wrath forever. / As far as the east is from the west, so far has he put our transgressions from us.*

Luke 15: 1-3, 11-32 Once more, Luke provides the context for us: *"The tax collectors and sinners were all gathering around Jesus to hear him, at which the Pharisees and the scribes murmured, 'This man welcomes sinners and eats with them.'"* So Jesus spins them a yarn about a man with two sons, whose younger son up and demands his share right now, so he can go off and start living la vida loca. Off he goes. But he and his new pals go through his stash real fast, and he ends up penniless, and of course suddenly friendless. Then, a famine breaks out. Goodby, frying pan. Hello, fire! He barely manages to get a job, but it's feeding (ugh) pigs—remember, the kid is Jewish. He's so broke he can't afford to buy any food, and he'd love to scarf up some of the pig-fare, but he doesn't dare. Then it hits him. Back home even the hired hands live better than this. *"I will return to my father and say to him, 'Father, I have sinned against God and against you; I no longer deserve to be called your son. Treat me like one of your hired hands.'"* And he sets off again. Meanwhile, back at the ranch, dad has been wistfully gazing into the distance, hoping against hope some day he'll see his boy again. Bingo! It's him! Dad is so happy he runs out to meet him and orders up fresh threads and some shots from that can of AXE in his brother's bathroom, so he can cut through the "scent" clinging to his boy.

Reflection:
A high-school English teacher once called this precious parable "the greatest short story of all time." Jesus shows his understanding of Micah's message by depicting the heavenly Father as this father, so prodigal in his pardon, so happy to welcome back. A telling detail: since Jesus gives us the young man's prepared speech, we see that the father's hug interrupts him; dad doesn't need to hear the full apology—it's enough that he has his son back, worn and rag-tag but safe. Let's party! Then, another sour note. The elder son resents the kid getting a party instead of a reprimand, so he could learn his lesson—and refuses to take part. So the father has to come outside and unruffle his feathers. He might well have added, "Just wait until you have kids, you'll see."

What a misnomer, to call the son prodigal because he was so generous with this money, and not the father, who was so generous with his love! Jesus is trying so hard to soften the hearts of the upright scribes and Pharisees, to get them to stop judging others and instead try to reach out to them in understanding and forgiveness. What a judge we have in Jesus!

And, by the way, what a chronicler we have in Luke, whose intent is so clearly to depict Jesus as the gentle, healing physician. Only in his gospel do we hear this story coming from deep in the heart of Jesus, nor does anyone else relate Jesus' words to the repentant thief crucified with him, "This day you will be with me in paradise." We are grateful to his editor, the Holy Spirit, for inspiring him to include these beauties.

Third Sunday of Lent

N.B. In parishes engaged in the Rite of Christian Initiation of
Adults (R.C.I.A.): readings for the Third, Fourth, and Fifth Sundays
of Lent are taken from Cycle A.

Cycle A – Scripture

Exodus 17: 3-7 *In their thirst the people grumbled against Moses, "Why
did you make us leave Egypt, just to have us die here of thirst with our
children and our livestock?" The Lord [told] Moses, "Holding the staff
with which you struck the river, strike the rock, and the water will flow
from it."*

Responsorial Psalm 95: 1-2, 6-7, 8-9

Romans 5: 1-2, 5-8 *The love of God has been poured out in our hearts
through the Holy Spirit who has been given to us. It is precisely in this
that God proves his loved for us: that while we were still sinners, Christ
died for us.*

John 4: 5-42 (shorter 4: 5-15, 19-26, 39, 40-42) At Jacob's Well, near
Shechem, Jesus asks a Samaritan woman to draw him some water. She
questions him in turn: how could he, a Jew, ask her, a Samaritan—and
a woman, to boot—to serve him? It was not seemly. Jesus fires back:
if you knew who this was talking to you, you'd be asking for a drink,
and he'd give you living water. Her comeback: you don't even have a
bucket, how can you talk about giving me any water? *The water I give
shall become a fountain within, leaping up to provide eternal life."* Then
gimme some, so I won't have to keep coming back here to get more.
Then we get into the "where's your husband" bit, and she becomes edgy
so she changes the subject to the old Jerusalem v. Samaria religious/
political debate. Jesus pounces and reveals himself as the expected

Messiah. She runs to town to share with them her conversation with the man, and the whole town comes back out with her, with many coming to accept and believe on her testimony and their own listening to Jesus.

Reflection:
Water is life, as life in a desert makes eminently clear. Moses brings the people life from God. But Jesus goes way beyond Moses. Speaking of the water at Jacob's Well, he says: *"Everyone who drinks this water will be thirsty again, but whoever drinks the water I give him will never be thirsty; no, the water I give shall become a fountain within him, leaping up to provide eternal life."* Jesus finds a way to have water, not brought to us, but springing up from within. And here's Paul's image: *"the love of God has been poured out in our hearts through the Holy Spirit who has been given to us."* Jesus is talking about a spiritual fountain, a bubbling spring of the Spirit producing life within us, even while we struggle against our death-dealing sins.

Third Sunday of Lent

Cycle B – Scripture

Exodus 20: 1-17 (shorter 20: 1-3, 7-8, 12-17) *God delivered all these commandments: I, the Lord am your God, who brought you out of the land of Egypt, that place of slavery.*
> *You shall not have other gods besides me.*
> *You shall not take the name of the Lord, your God, in vain.*
> *Remember to keep holy the Sabbath day.*
> *Honor your father and your mother.*
> *You shall not kill.*
> *You shall not commit adultery.*
> *You shall not steal.*
> *You shall not bear false witness against your neighbor.*
> *You shall not covet your neighbor's house, nor wife, nor slave,*
> *nor anything else that belongs to him.*

Responsorial Psalm 19: 8, 9, 10, 11

1 Corinthians 1: 22-25 *Jews demand "signs" and Greeks look for "wisdom," but we preach Christ crucified, a stumbling block to Jews, and an absurdity to Gentiles; but to those who are called, Jews and Greeks alike, Christ is the power of God and the wisdom of God. For God's folly is wiser than men, and his weakness more powerful than men.*

John 2: 13-25 Jesus went to Jerusalem for the Passover. In the temple area he found people selling animals and others changing coins. He made a whip and drove them all out, knocking down the money-changers' tables with all their coins. He told them: Get out of here, and stop turning my Father's house into a marketplace! The Jews demanded to know on what authority he did these things, and he answered: *Destroy this temple and in three days I will raise it up.* They retorted: *This temple took forty-six years to build, and you are going to raise it up in three days!* But it turns out Jesus was talking about the temple of his body. Later, after he had been raised from the dead, his disciples recalled how he had said this.

Reflection:
The Exodus reading has the Israelites on Mount Sinai; they have escaped from Egypt under the leadership of Moses, who now receives from the Lord the commandments they are to observe as their part of the saving covenant with God. In the New Covenant Jesus will fulfill and leave behind the commandments, teaching us to surpass the mere minimal obligations of the law in order to fulfill the constant invitations of love that God sends our way. We shouldn't worry about not keeping the laws—we should worry about not doing enough good! (Or have we forgotten Matthew 25?)

A Christ crucified, as opposed to victorious and glorious, does not fit the mind-set of Jewish expectations of the Messiah, and seems folly rather than wisdom to the Greeks with their reliance on what seems reasonable, logical to them. But when you think about it, there would be more wisdom in the folly of God than there could be in all the best thinking of the wisest of men. It may not make sense in the world to stop and help others—it means you're losing your place in the race! For Christians, however, stopping to help others is precisely the path Jesus points out and demonstrates for us to follow. Jesus has already saved our places; we are now free to devote ourselves to others instead of obsessing about ourselves.

Jesus can't stand what they've made of his Father's holy house: a marketplace, a 4-H exhibition hall, a money-changers' meeting place, with guys hanging around gossiping. I love how he makes sure to tip over their tables, so they have to go chasing after all those coins rolling around under everything. His disciples, in awe, would recall the Scripture: "Zeal for your house consumes me." Jesus takes off the gloves— this is going to be bare-knuckled. No more Mr. Nice Guy. The hostility between him and his enemies is open and obvious, on both sides. Does he flinch? Does he worry about threats to his safety? He's in this for us, so he carries on bravely. Our response to this awesome selfless love? Think about it…then do something about it. (Hint: love one another as I have loved you.)

Third Sunday of Lent

Cycle C – Scripture

Exodus 3: 1-8, 13-15 Moses was tending his father-in-law's flock when he came to Horeb, the mountain of God. An angel of the Lord appeared to Moses in fire flaming out of a bush that, although it burned, was not consumed by the flames. God called out to him from the bush: *"Come no nearer! Remove the sandals from your feet, for the place where you stand is holy ground. I am the God of Abraham, Isaac [and] Jacob."* Moses hid his face; he was afraid to look at God. But the Lord said, *"I have witnessed the affliction of my people in Egypt and have heard their cry. Therefore I have come to rescue them from the Egyptians and lead them into a land flowing with milk and honey."* Moses is still gun-shy and raises an objection. *"When I go to the Israelites and say: 'the God of your fathers has sent me to you,' if they ask me, 'What is his name?' what am I to tell them?"* God replied, *"I am who am."* Almost as if he sensed how strange this might sound, he adds, *"You shall tell [them]: I AM sent me to you."*

Responsorial Psalm 103: 1-2, 3-4, 6-7, 8, 11

1 Corinthians 10: 1-6, 10-12 *Our fathers all passed through the sea; by the sea all of them were baptized into Moses. Yet we know that God was not pleased with most of them, for "they were struck down in the desert." These things happened as an example to keep us from wicked desires such as theirs [and] have been written as a warning to us. Let anyone who thinks he is standing upright watch out lest he fall!*

Luke 13: 1-9 Jesus makes reference to a toppled tower that killed eighteen people—it must have been on CNN, his listeners all know about it—to make his point: you think those eighteen deserved to die any more than the rest of the injured? Then he answers his own question: *"Certainly not! But I tell you, you will all come to the same end unless you begin to reform."* So, to drive home the need for preparedness, for beginning to reform RIGHT NOW, he tells them a parable about a man who had a fig tree in his vineyard, and kept looking for fruit on it but never found any. He said to the vinedresser, "For three years now I've been coming for fruit on this fig tree and never found any. Cut it down. Why should it take up space?" The man said, *"Sir, leave it another year while I hoe around it and manure it; then perhaps it will bear fruit. If not, it shall be cut down."*

Reflection:
I have always found it difficult to read this passage aloud: "I am who am" is an awkward phrase, it doesn't roll gracefully off the lips. And isn't it supremely fitting that the expression of this concept is every bit as

difficult as the understanding of it? Let's face it, we're not ever going to get a handle on God, we're finite. He's entirely beyond us, this Transcendent Being, this great "I AM" in capital letters. Isaiah 45:22 quotes him, "I am God—there is no other!" Just to say his name is a humbling experience for us…and that is as it should be. No wonder when the Jews read Yahweh (God) with their eyes they pronounced Adonai (Lord) with their lips—he is so sacred even his name is beyond us.

[A historical note: this respectful reluctance to pronounce the sacred name, the very definition of a reverential "fear of the Lord," is what opens the door to the variant "Jehovah" used by some Christians. Jewish writing consisted of only consonants, they figured any reader could supply the missing vowels as he went along. Some manuscripts tried to make it easier for the reader and included, not letters, but little markings below the consonants to refer to the missing vowels. "Jehovah" results when the vowel markings for "Adonai" appear below the YHWH of "Yahweh," producing what would sound like "Yahowah," unless you remembered you were supposed to pronounce "Adonai." By 1530, when this variant first appears, it's been a millennium and a half since we split off from our Jewish roots, and nearly twice that long since anybody had actually heard the word pronounced. Now back to our regular programming….]

Paul reminds us to not take our salvation for granted. Just being baptized is no guarantee. Don't make the same mistakes the Israelites did. And don't get cocky! But live prudently in the Spirit, close to Christ.

Jesus also sounds a warning note: you'd better begin to reform, because you don't know what's going to happen to you. You think the victims of that fallen tower deserved that fate more than those who weren't killed? It just happened, so heads up! The lesson in his parable is the same: don't miss your chance to begin yielding fruit for God, because he might be getting tired of waiting.

Third Week of Lent

OPTIONAL MASS for any weekday of the Third Week of Lent, especially in the years of Cycles B or C. On a Cycle A year, the gospel appears on the Third Sunday of Lent.

Cycle A – Scripture

Exodus 17: 1-7 The Israelites have left Egypt behind, but now they have no water! They quarrel with Moses: *What shall I do with this people? A little more and they will stone me!* The Lord assures Moses he will provide the water: *I will be standing in front of you on the rock in Horeb. Strike the rock, and the water will flow from it for the people to drink.*
Responsorial Psalm 95: 1-2, 6-7, 8-9

John 4: 5-42 This gospel appeared at Mass of the Third Sunday of Lent, Cycle A, p. 36.

Reflection:
Water is a favorite symbol for the life of grace, provided by God in one case from the rock, in the other from within!

Monday Third Week

Scripture

2Kings 5: 1-15 Naaman, the brave and successful army commander of the king of Aram (Syria), was nonetheless a leper. In one of his raids he had captured a young Israelite girl, who became the servant of his wife. She told her, "If only your husband would present himself to the prophet in Samaria, he could cure him of his leprosy." Naaman passed this report to his king, who retorted, "Go, I will send along a letter to the king of Israel." So Naaman set out, taking along silver, and gold, and festal garments. To the king of Israel he brought the letter, which read: "With this letter I am sending my servant Naaman to you, that you may cure him of his leprosy."

When he read the letter, the king of Israel tore his garments: "Am I a god with power over life and death, that the king should send me someone to be cured of leprosy? Check it out! He's just looking to start something!" When Elisha, the man of God, heard of it, he sent word to his king: "Why did you tear your garments? Send him to me so he'll find out that there is a prophet in Israel." Naaman came to the door of Elisha's house. The prophet didn't even bother coming to the door, he just sent word: "Go and wash seven times in the Jordan and you will be clean." Naaman was upset, and said "I figured he would come out and invoke the Lord his God, and at least move his hand over the spot, and remove my leprosy. Besides, aren't the rivers of Damascus, back home, better than all the waters of Israel? Could I not wash in them and be cleaned?" He turned about in anger and started to leave. But his servants reasoned with him: "If the prophet had told you to do something weird and strange, wouldn't you have done it? All he said was 'Wash,' so why don't you?" So Naaman plunged into the Jordan seven times, and his flesh became clean again. He returned to Elisha and said "Now I know that there is no God in all the earth, except in Israel."

Responsorial Psalm 42: 2, 3; 43: 3, 4

Luke 4: 24-30 *When Jesus had come to Nazareth, he said to the people in the synagogue: "No prophet gains acceptance in his native place. There were many widows in Israel in the days of Elijah [but] it was to none of these that Elijah was sent, but to a widow of Zarephath near Sidon. Recall the many lepers in Israel in the time of Elisha the prophet, yet not one was cured except Naaman the Syrian." At these words the whole audience was filled with indignation, rose up and expelled him from the town intending to hurl him over the edge [of the hill].*

Reflection:
Notice Naaman's natural reaction: "First, he doesn't even come down the steps to greet me, then he sends his servant with these silly instructions. And I've got better rivers back home than this stupid Jordan of his." Thank God his servants convince him with their sensible thinking. And, in the end, what a marvelous result and return to the prophet, who this time, obviously, is there to greet him and rejoice with him.

And, for Jesus, a narrow escape. The irony of Israel's God being acknowledged by the Syrian general (the outsider who recognizes the truth) deepens and becomes menacing as Jesus feels firsthand the rejection that will intensify and extend, from his home town (the insiders who reject the truth), to the once-welcoming crowds in Jerusalem soon after Palm Sunday's triumphant entry.

Tuesday Third Week

Scripture

Daniel 3: 25, 34-43 *Azariah stood up in the fire and prayed aloud: "For your name's sake, O Lord, do not deliver us up forever. For we are reduced, O Lord, beyond any other nation. We have in our day no prince, prophet, or leader, no sacrifice, oblation or incense, no place to offer first fruits, to find favor with you. But with contrite heart and humble spirit let us be received as though it were holocausts of rams and bullocks, or thousands of fat lambs. Deliver us by your wonders, and bring glory to your name, O Lord."*

Responsorial Psalm 25: 4-5, 6-7, 8-9

Matthew 18: 21-35 When Peter asked Jesus, "When my brother wrongs me, how often must I forgive him? Seven times?" and the answer comes, "seventy times seven times," that would be (to an unschooled mind) an exponential jump. You just don't keep score, you'll run out of numbers. So Jesus gives a clear, non-academic example: "The reign of God is like a king who decided to settle accounts with his officials." One owed him a gazillion dollars, from loans he kept promising to repay, but there was no way he could, so his master ordered him sold, and his wife and kids, and all his property, to get back as much as he could on the debt. When he said, "My lord, be patient with me and I will pay you back in full," he felt sorry for him and said, "Fuhgetaboutit!"

But when that same official met a fellow servant who owed him a couple of bucks for the lunch he had to buy one day at the cafeteria, he grabbed him by the neck and demanded full repayment. Now the man pleaded with him in almost the exact same words: "Just give me time and I will pay you back in full." But he wasn't interested. He called the collection agency had him put in jail until he paid back what he owed. His fellow servants saw what had happened and were so shaken that they reported the whole incident to their master. He sent for him and said, "You louse, you worthless wretch! I canceled your entire debt when you pleaded with me. Shouldn't you have dealt mercifully with your fellow servant, as I dealt with you?" And in anger he handed him over to the torturers. Moral of the story: my heavenly Father will treat you in exactly the same way unless each of you forgives his brother from his heart.

Reflection:

When it seems we have nothing (no thing) to offer God, let us remember he doesn't want anything (any thing) from us. He doesn't want an offering to burn at an altar to buy his favor, but a humble spirit and a contrite heart to approach him in confidence, so he can pick us up and set us back on the right path. "Do not let us be put to shame," we beg him, acknowledging our guilt, "but deal with us in your kindness and great mercy."

But we can't ask him for mercy if we don't act mercifully ourselves. This is one of my favorite parables of the Lord, because it is so simply and powerfully played out. The moral (and he doesn't always include one, so he must not want us to miss this one) is also simple but quite powerful.

Next time you pray the Lord's Prayer, think about what you're asking for…and what you can do about it.

Wednesday Third Week

Scripture

Deuteronomy 4: 1, 5-9 *Israel, hear the statutes and decrees which I am teaching you to observe, that you may live, and may enter in and take possession of the land which the Lord, the God of your fathers, is giving you. The nations will hear of all these statutes and say, "This great nation is truly a wise and intelligent people." Take care not to let them slip from your memory as long as you live, but teach them to your children and to your children's children.*

Responsorial Psalm 147: 12-13, 15-16, 19-20

Matthew 5: 17-19 *I have come, not to abolish [the law and the prophets] but to fulfill them. Whoever breaks the least significant of these commands and teaches others to do so shall be called least in the kingdom of God. Whoever fulfills and teaches these commands shall be great in the kingdom of God.*

Reflection:
In the early Church, the liturgy of the word of the Masses of this season was used to gather and educate those interested in becoming Christians with us. (Successful completion would be celebrated by the initiation rites of the Holy Saturday Night Mass, the Vigil of Easter: Baptism, Confirmation, First Eucharist.) Every so often they held a scrutiny, a test, of how they were coming along. This mass is obviously a test of the catechumens' grasp of their basic tenets, the commandments.

The first reading is Moses pumping up his people, pointing out that no one else had such a bond, such a closeness to their God, since they were covenanted to him by their observance of these laws. We live by these laws and God gives us our freedom in these lands!

And Jesus pumps up his listeners by assuring them he'll make it his business to fulfill every little expectation of the law. In fact, he'll go on to surpass it, by not limiting himself to the letter of the law, but giving attention also to the spirit in which it was given. Recall all his teachings which go: "You've heard it said…but I tell you…."

Thursday Third Week

Scripture

Jeremiah 7: 23-28 *Thus says the Lord: Listen to my voice, then I will be your God and you will be my people. But they turned their backs, not their faces, to me. From the day your fathers left Egypt even to this day, I have sent you untiringly my prophets. Yet they have not paid heed. They will not listen to you either. Faithfulness has disappeared; the word itself is banished from their speech.*

Responsorial Psalm 95: 1-2, 6-7, 8-9

Luke 11: 14-23 *Jesus was casting out a devil which was mute, and the dumb man spoke. The crowds were amazed. Some said, "It is by Beelzebul, the prince of devils, that he casts out devils." Jesus said, "If Satan is divided against himself, how can his kingdom last?—since you say it is by Beelzebul that I cast out devils. But if it is by the finger of God that I cast out devils, then the reign of God is upon you.*

Reflection:
Jeremiah had a tough time, and God knew what the prophet was up against—although that didn't stop him from sending the prophet back up to the plate for a few more cuts. What sadness in the redundant but heart-rending line, "the word itself is banished." And the image of backs instead of faces comes from a world where the local Arab sheik could have your head cut off if you turned to leave his presence instead of bowing and clumsily but respectfully maintaining that bow while you exited his tent! What an insult…and to such a loving God!

And the insults continue: Jesus is accused of using the devil's power in his miracles. Ugh! But he keeps his cool and counters with logic, plain and simple. Could his power not be coming from the God in whose name he so clearly speaks and acts? Remember him making just these points? When you hear me, you hear the one who sent me. If you don't believe my words, then believe the works that you see me doing. I do the work of my Father. God sent a lot more than his word to us in this prophet—he sent the Word made Flesh, a walking/ talking audiovisual of Himself for all the world to see and hear!

Friday Third Week

Scripture

Hosea 14: 2-10 *Return, O Israel, to the Lord, your God. Say to him, "Forgive all iniquity. We shall say no more, 'Our god,' to the work of our hands; for in you the orphan finds compassion." I will heal their defection, I will love them freely; for my wrath is turned from them. I will be like dew for Israel: he shall blossom like the lily.*

Responsorial Psalm 81: 6-8, 8-9, 10-11, 14, 17

Mark 12: 28-34 *The scribe said to [Jesus], "Excellent, Teacher! You are right in saying, 'He is the One, there is no other than he.' Yes, 'to love him with all our heart, with all our thoughts and with all our strength, and to love our neighbor as ourselves' is worth more than any burnt offering or sacrifice." Jesus approved the insight of this answer and told him, "You are not far from the reign of God."*

Reflection:
No prophet preaches more powerfully about God's love for us than Hosea. His God longs for our return, pleads for it, opens the way…like a husband who thinks back to a magical honeymoon in Hawaii and says "maybe all we need is a few days in the islands again…." The Hebrew hesed translates as "tender love," the hallmark of Yahweh's approach to his people: like dew bringing a lily to blossom.

This selection of Mark's Gospel notes the genuine interest of the questioner—gone is the usual "and, to test him, asked…." Jesus' answer strikes an enthusiastic chord in the scribe, and Jesus is quick to encourage his interest. What a beautiful insight the scribe gained: love (of God and of neighbor) means so much more than any offering or sacrifice!

Makes you wonder: who came up with that "I love you so much you can have my favorite (fill in the blank)"? I know, it's a reflection of the greater value that we're placing on the target of our gift…but so easily the gift can end up not just representing us, but actually taking our place, so that we no longer enter into the exchange, only our gift does. No wonder so many times we hear, "give me your hearts, not your burnt offerings! Don't impress me; I don't need your gifts, I need you!" Brings to mind that starkly impressive but awful story from the Book of Judges about Jephthah promising God the sacrifice of the first person he meets on his victorious return home from battle (figuring it would be one of his servants, most likely)—and it turns out to be his only child (11:29ff).

Saturday Third Week

Scripture

Hosea 6: 1-6 *What can I do with you, Ephraim? What can I do with you, Judah? Your piety is like the dew that early passes away. For this reason I smote them through the prophets, I slew them by the words of my mouth. For it is love that I desire, not sacrifice, and knowledge of God rather than holocausts.*

Responsorial Psalm 51: 3-4, 18-19, 20-21 *For you are not pleased with sacrifices; should I offer a holocaust, you would not accept it. My sacrifice, O God, is a contrite spirit; a heart contrite and humbled, O God, you will not spurn.*

Luke 18: 9-14 *Two men went up to the temple to pray: a Pharisee [and] a tax collector. The Pharisee took up his position and spoke this prayer to himself: "I give you thanks, O God, that I am not like the rest of men—grasping, crooked, adulterous—or even like this tax collector." The other man, however, not even daring to raise his eyes to heaven, beat his breast and [said], "O God, be merciful to me, a sinner." Believe me, this man went home justified, but the other did not.*

Reflection:

In the Scriptures, Ephraim is synonymous with the ten northern tribes, Judah with the southern two. How strong is God's reprimand for the shallow response he receives from his people—he smites them with the words of his prophets. What else can he do? He's at a loss in his attempts to elicit a meaningful, personal response to the deep love he keeps offering us. The psalmist shows his insight, in one of his most intense penitential prayers: "in the greatness of your compassion wipe out my offense, and of my sin cleanse me; my sacrifice is a contrite spirit, a heart contrite and humbled."

Luke frames this parable precisely, pointing out that Jesus addressed it "to those who believed in their own self-righteousness," and if that were not enough, "while holding everyone else in contempt." No wonder there's a tradition that Luke was an artist, when we see his masterful inclusion of such telling physical details as "took up his position" and "not even daring to raise his eyes to heaven." Talk about "body language."

It's pretty clear to the listener that one was just "doing business," dictating a letter, center stage, while the other was not giving a thought to how he was doing, but concentrating wholly on the merciful God whose pardon he was seeking. Hmm…where are our minds, and hearts, when we pray?

Fourth Sunday of Lent

Cycle A – Scripture

1 Samuel 16: 1, 6-7, 10-13 *The Lord said to Samuel: "I am sending you to Jesse of Bethlehem, for I have chosen my king from among his sons." Samuel looked at Eliab [the first-born] and thought "Surely the Lord's anointed is here." But the Lord said to Samuel: "Do not judge from his appearance, because not as man sees does God see; man sees the appearance but the Lord looks into the heart." [Eventually, David appears] and the Lord says, "There—anoint him, for this is he!" And from that day on, the spirit of the Lord rushed upon David.*

Responsorial Psalm 23: 1-3, 3-4, 5, 6

Ephesians 5: 8-14 *There was a time when you were in darkness, but now you are light in the Lord. Well, then, live as children of light.*

John 9: 1-41 (shorter 9: 1, 6-9, 13-17, 34-38) When they came upon a man who was blind from birth, Jesus' disciples asked whose sin caused this: his, or his parents'? Neither, is his answer, *"rather, it was to let God's works show forth in him. We must do the deeds of him who sent me while it is day. The night comes on when no one can work. While I am in the world, I am the light of the world."* Jesus smeared the man's eyes and sent him to wash in the Pool of Siloam. He went, he washed, he saw!

The regulars began to ask: Isn't that the guy who used to sit and beg? They weren't sure, given the change. But he said, I'm the one! How'd it happen? A man they call Jesus made some mud and smeared my eyes, then he sent me to wash, and bingo! They asked: So where is he? I should know? Duh! I've never seen him before in my life. Then they took him to the authorities, the Pharisees (maybe because it was on a Sabbath that all this happened?) who asked him for his story. Some of them said about Jesus: This man cannot be from God because he does not keep the Sabbath. (Did I tell you?) Others, God bless them, pointed out that if Jesus were such a sinner, how could God have worked this miracle through him? So they turned back to the man and asked: You're the guy he healed…what do you think? I think he's a prophet, he answered.

The Jews simply refused to believe Jesus could pull this off, so they sent to ask the blind man's parents if in fact he had been born blind. They knew their answer would not please the authorities, so they said: He's old enough to answer for himself; ask him. Which they did, opening with this remark: we know this man is a sinner. He came back: Well, I wouldn't know if he was a sinner or not; all I know is that he cured my blindness. How? Why do you want to hear it again? I've already told you…are you thinking of becoming his disciples? Hey—you're this man's follower. We are disciples of Moses. Where this man comes from we have no idea. He said: Isn't that something? Here you don't know where he comes from, yet I know for a fact that God wouldn't listen to a sinner in granting such a cure as mine. They grew angry at this—how dare you preach to us—and threw him out bodily.

52

Later, Jesus sought him out and introduced himself to him. The man bowed down to thank and worship Jesus, who said: "*I came into this world to divide it, to make the sightless see and the seeing blind.*" Pharisees nearby (and weren't they always?) heard him and asked whether he was including them with the blind. Jesus answered, "*If you were blind there would be no sin*" —you'd have an excuse for not knowing, but since you keep insisting that you are not blind, that makes you guilty, so your sin remains.

Reflection:

This whole Sunday's readings make one long and wonderful commentary on Jesus our Light. No coincidence that it falls on <u>Laetare</u> Sunday, when the Church gladdens us with the message to hang in there, to take a breather from the long pull of penitential Sundays. The first reading reminds us how different God's view of things is from our view. We get distracted by externals, he sees right into the heart of things. We <u>think</u> we see, but we are blind to the truth of what's out there. Paul's masterful images drive his point home: we once were in darkness, but now we are light in the Lord. Notice—not <u>in</u> the light, but more properly, we have become light in Christ! <u>with</u> Christ! Then John's gospel presents a lengthy but always interesting (sparkling dialog!) account of Jesus giving sight to one born blind—obviously a very telling point, that the man never had the sight that Jesus brings to him. This is no restoring of a human ability to see, this is a bringing into the light!

Fourth Sunday of Lent

Cycle B – Scripture

2 Chronicles 36: 14-17, 19-23 All the princes of Judah, the priests and the people added infidelity to infidelity, practicing all the abominations of the nations and polluting the Lord's temple which he had consecrated in Jerusalem. God had compassion on them, and kept sending them messengers, but to no avail. They scoffed at his prophets and despised his warnings. So he let them have it. Jerusalem fell, totally and igno-miniously. The temple was burned, the walls torn down, their palaces set afire, and those who escaped with their lives were taken captive to Babylon to become slaves. Eventually, in accord with Jeremiah's word, when Cyrus of Persia overcomes the Babylonians they are released and return home.

Responsorial Psalm 137: 1-2, 3, 4-5, 6

Ephesians 2: 4-10 *God is rich in mercy; because of his great love for us he brought us to life with Christ when we were dead in sin. This is not your own doing; it is God's gift; neither is it a reward for anything you have accomplished.*

John 3: 14-21 *Just as Moses lifted up the serpent in the desert, so must the Son of Man be lifted up, that all who believe may have eternal life in him. Yes, God so loved the world that he gave his only Son, that whoever believes in him may not die but may have eternal life. God did not send the Son into the world to condemn the world, but that the world might be saved through him.*

Reflection:
It's a morally decrepit scenario. Abominations are taking place in God's holy temple, and by the hands of his own people. Prophets are sent to stop the abuses, but time and time again they are ignored and ridiculed. Enough! God uses the Babylonian Empire to overthrow and demolish Jerusalem, and the leaders of the people are taken away as slaves. Hard times make for re-evaluation, which leads to repentance. Eventually, after being force-fed a chance to get straight, they receive their reprieve and return home. How apt is Paul's description, "when we were dead in sin." But God's love found a way to allow us a new beginning, we are brought to life in Christ Jesus, not through any merit of our own, but because of God's great and merciful love, extended to us despite our behavior.

The third selection's theme is the same: from death to life. No wonder this falls on <u>Laetare</u> Sunday, the church's rest-stop in our long haul following Christ from suffering, through death, to his new life. It is news to make us glad: that God chooses consistently to put our sins behind us as he offers yet another chance for us to come close to him and (this time) <u>stay there!</u> Remember the incident of the poisonous snakes in the desert with their burning bites? (They were called seraph snakes because of the fire of their bite.) When Moses relayed the people's conversion and renewed loyalty, Yahweh instructed him to hoist a bronze snake on a pole, so that all who looked on it would be healed by their contrition. Jesus will use this symbol in speaking of his crucifixion. I was not sent to condemn the world, but to save it. So look on this symbol of human defeat and see what it truly is—the instrument of your salvation.

Fourth Sunday of Lent

Cycle C – Scripture

Joshua 5: 9, 10-12 *The Lord said to Joshua, "Today I have removed the reproach of Egypt from you." While the Israelites were encamped at Gilgal, they celebrated the Passover on the evening of the fourteenth of the month. On the day after Passover they ate of the produce of the land [and] the manna ceased.*

Responsorial Psalm 34: 2-3, 4-5, 6-7

2Corinthians 5: 17-21 *If anyone is in Christ, he is a new creation. The old order has passed away; now all is new! God has reconciled us to himself through Christ and has given us the ministry of reconciliation. For our sakes God made him who did not know sin to be sin, so that in him we might become the very holiness of God.*

Luke 15: 1-3, 11-32 (The parable of the Prodigal Son has appeared and been reflected on already in the Gospel selection for the mass of Saturday of the Second Week of Lent, p. 34.)

Reflection:

The providential bread from heaven which the Israelites received in the desert on a daily basis–it would be spoil overnight if they tried to hoard it–taught them to trust in God's care and to rely on him rather than on their own power ("give us this day our daily bread"). When he brought them into their own land, where they were able to settle and grow their own food, the miraculous feedings came to an end, like a mother weaning her child when it can handle "postgraduate" chow. For Christians, the connection with the Passover is super-obvious. We recall Jesus celebrating just that feast and taking bread into his holy hands and breaking it for his disciples at table with him. And we also recall, "I am the true bread from heaven. Your fathers ate manna in the desert, but they died. Anyone who eats my flesh and drinks my blood will live forever."

In his great mercy, our God has chosen to reconcile us through Christ, making it possible for us to begin anew: our transgressions have been control-alt-delete'd; there's not a mark left on us. What a beautiful reprieve, the release from our past burdens. If we know this wonderful feeling, then we know what we're supposed to do about it—spread it to others, as we reconcile with one another and lift the burdens of guilt and shame from each other, just as Christ has done for us.

We have visited the power-filled final line, verse 21 of our second reading, already on Ash Wednesday: "For our sakes God made him who did not know sin to be sin, so that in him we might become the very holiness of God." What a startling concept, that God made the sinless Jesus to be sin so that, by a marvelous osmosis, we sinners could take on his holiness! I am happy, every time I celebrate the Eucharist, to make an equally daring and startling request as I mingle the inert, lame drops of water with the potent, vigorous wine in the chalice as I prepare the gifts at the Offertory: "By the mystery of this water and wine, may we come to share in the [holy, powerful] divinity of Christ, who humbled himself to share in our [weak, sinful] humanity." Holy Osmosis, Batman!

With all this good stuff happening (manna in the desert, harvests in their new land, total removal of sins through reconciliation and re-creation in Christ, the son who was lost but came back to life) we're not surprised to see the celebrant walk out for Mass vested in rose garments rather than the familiar penitential purple of the season. It's Take-a-Break Sunday, when mother Church feels we could use a breather in the long and difficult haul begun over three weeks ago. Remember "Gaudete (Rejoice!) Sunday" halfway through the season of Advent? Same deal: now it's "Laetare (Be Glad!) Sunday" we're given as a rest-stop on our Lenten journey with Christ, from suffering to glory.

SOLEMNITY OF SAINT JOSEPH (floater: March 19th)

2Samuel 7: 4-5. 12-14, 16 *The Lord spoke to Nathan and said, "Tell my servant David 'When you rest with your ancestors, I will raise up your heir after you. I will be a father to him, and he shall be a son to me. Your house and your kingdom will endure forever.' "*

Responsorial Psalm 89: 2-3. 4-5, 27, 29 *I have made a covenant with my chosen one, I have sworn to David my servant: forever I will maintain my kindness toward him, and my covenant with him stands firm.*

Romans 4: 13, 16-18, 22 *Hoping against hope, Abraham believed [what] was once told him, "Numerous as this [the stars in the sky] shall your descendants be." Thus his faith was credited to him as justice.*

Matthew 1: 16, 18-21, 24 Joseph found out Mary was pregnant while they were engaged, but before they lived together. Being a decent chap, he decided to divorce her quietly and not cause her any trouble, when suddenly the angel of the Lord appeared to him in a dream and said, "Have no fear about taking Mary as your wife. It is by the Holy Spirit that she has conceived this child, a son whom you are to name Jesus because he will save his people from their sins." When Joseph awoke he received her into his home as his wife.

(alternate) **Luke 2: 41-52** The parents of Jesus used to go every year to Jerusalem for the Passover, and when he was twelve, as they were returning home, he remained behind, unknown to his parents. They returned to Jerusalem after searching for him three days, and found him in the temple sitting with the elders, listening and asking questions. Impressive, but disturbing nonetheless. His mother said, "Son, why have you done this to us? We have been searching for you in sorrow." He said, "Why? Did you not know I had to be in my Father's house?" His mother kept all these things in memory.

Reflection:
Through the prophet Nathan, God promises David, his chosen one, that his line will continue forever. A special, tender relationship is evident between them: "I will be a father to him, and he shall be a son to me." Psalm 89 elucidates, in David's words.

Paul consistently puts faith ahead of observance of the Law. "Certainly the promise to Abraham did not depend on the law; it was made in view of the justice that comes from faith. All depends on faith, everything is a grace." Abraham's faith, so dramatically tested by the request for the sacrifice of his only son, was "credited to him as justice."

Matthew's gospel situates Jesus as the promised Christ (Messiah) as he tells of Joseph acting as Jesus' legal father and adopting him into the royal Davidic line. This is more important than it might seem at first glance: Jesus the son of Mary has no legal standing in Jewish patriarchal society; Jesus the son of Joseph as Mary's husband belongs to the royal family's promised never-ending kingship.

In Luke's gospel selection Jesus is surprisingly causing his parents anguish, of all things! On one of their yearly visits to Jerusalem to celebrate the Passover (good family custom) he stays behind to join a group of teachers in discussion. "How could you do this to us? How could you cause us this sorrow?" "Where else would I be but in my Father's house?" Luke has Mary keeping "all these things" in her heart. And if he weren't so darned taken up with her (his Gentile background prompts him to disregard the patriarchal preponderance of the Jews— Title IX rules!) he might well have added, "And his father wondered what he had gotten into, and what kind of a man Jesus would turn out to be."

OPTIONAL MASS any weekday of the Fourth Week of Lent, especially in the years of a B or C Cycle. On a Cycle A year, the gospel appears on the Fourth Sunday of Lent.

Fourth Week of Lent

Scripture

Micah 7:7-9 *I will look to the Lord, my God will hear me! Though I sit in darkness, the Lord is my light. He will bring me forth to the light; I will see his justice.*

Responsorial Psalm 27: 1, 7-8, 8-9, 13-14

John 9: 1-41 This gospel was proclaimed on the Fourth Sunday of Lent, p. 51.

Reflection:
Christ is the light of the soul being brought out of the darkness of sin; he removes our blindness to the presence of his love in our lives. The Pool of Siloam prefigures the waters of baptism.

Monday Fourth Week

Scripture

Isaiah 65: 17-21 *I am about to create new heavens and a new earth; the things of the past shall not be remembered. Instead there shall always be rejoicing in what I create. For I create Jerusalem to be a joy; no longer shall the sound of weeping be heard there. They shall live in the houses they build, and eat the fruit of the vineyards they plant.*

Responsorial Psalm 30: 2, 4, 5-6, 11-13

John 4:43-54 *At Capernaum there was a royal official whose son was ill. He begged Jesus to come and restore [his] health, [he] was near death. Jesus replied, "Unless you people see signs and wonders, you do not believe." "Sir," the official pleaded, "come down before my child dies." Jesus told him, "Return home. Your son will live." The man put his trust in Jesus and started for home. On his way, his servants met him [and said] his boy was going to live. When he asked what time the boy had [improved] they told him, "Yesterday afternoon about one." It was at that very hour, the father realized, that Jesus had told him, "Your son is going to live." He and his whole household became believers.*

Reflection:

The rosy glow of <u>Laetare</u> Sunday's Mass carries over to today. Good news for Jerusalem! The Lord will re-create it so that only joy, no more weeping, will be their lot. They are assured of that most basic Old Testament promise of stability and happiness: what they build they will inhabit (not lose it to conquering enemies), and what they plant they shall harvest (not some usurper who helps himself to the fruit of their efforts). And great news for the royal official! His persistence overcomes Jesus' seeming reluctance, and when he realizes the power of the Lord's healing word ("at that very hour") his response is joyously wholehearted. Kind of reminds you of the "born again" stories with their dramatic, life-changing, never-to-be-forgotten incidents. If the typical Catholic feels left out for lack of a similarly crucial event, we should remember all the non-dramatic, everyday wonders that visit us in the reception of Jesus at Communion at every Mass, the moments of inspiration by the Holy Spirit's prompting of our conscience, the felt joy in a beauteous celebration of a special liturgy, as in the washing of each other's feet on a Holy Thursday, or the welcoming of new Christians on a Holy Saturday night.

Tuesday Fourth Week

Scripture

Ezekiel 47: 1-9, 12 The angel brought me to the entrance of the temple of the Lord, and I saw water flowing out from beneath the threshold. He took me outside, and then he measured off a thousand cubits and had me wade through the water, which was ankle-deep. Another thousand cubits and once more he had me wade through the water, which was now knee-deep. Again a thousand and the water came up to my waist. Once more a thousand, but now it was river through which I could not wade; I had to swim to get across it. Then he brought me to the bank of the river, and told me to sit and look around. I saw very many trees on both banks, and he said, "This water flows and empties into the sea's salty waters, making them fresh. Along both banks fruit trees of every kind shall grow; their leaves won't wilt, nor will their fruit fail. Every month they shall bear fresh fruit, for they shall be watered by the flow from the sanctuary. Their fruit shall serve for food, and their leaves for medicine."

Responsorial Psalm 46: 2-3, 5-6, 8-9

John 5: 1-3, 5-16 In Jerusalem by the Sheep Pool there is a place with the Hebrew name Bethesda. Its porticos were crowded with sick people lying there blind, lame or disabled. One poor old sick man had been there for thirty-eight years. Jesus knew he had been sick a long time, and asked him "Do you want to be healed?" "Sir," he answered, "I don't have anyone to plunge me into the pool once the water has been stirred up. By the time I get myself there, someone else always beats me to it." Jesus ordered him, "Stand up, pick up your mat and walk!" Problem solved. The man was cured that instant, and picked up his mat and began to walk off…well, maybe he was skipping.

This happened on a Sabbath, so some of the Jews remarked, "Hey, what are you doing? You're not allowed to carry that around." "The man who cured me told me to pick it up and walk." "What man?" He had no idea who it was because it was so crowded that Jesus had been able to slip away. Later, Jesus found him in the temple precincts and told him: "Remember, you have been cured. Give up your sins so that something worse won't happen to you." The man went off and informed the Jews that Jesus was the one who had cured him. And it was because Jesus did things like this on the Sabbath that they began to persecute him.

Reflection:
Fresh, flowing water was the necessity for a desert people. It meant their life. Daniel's vision, then, points to God's temple as the source of his people's life. What a beautifully arranged telling of the tale. First, a trickle, then more and more and more, until it reaches the sea, whose salty waters it freshens. There's no stopping it—even the sea cannot prevail against it! Not only that, but along the way it waters both banks so that trees yield fruit of every kind, and—check it out: they bear every month! Talk about fertile, life-filled growth. But, (like an early version of the Popeil TV pitch), that's not all! Even the leaves serve for medicine. Whoa, Nellie! I get the feeling Smetana had Daniel's vision in mind when he traced "The Moldau" from its playful bubbling-spring source to its slow, majestic entry into the sea.

John's gospel completes this "Water of Life Mass." It seems the Sheep Pool was famous for miraculous healings: the first one in after an angel from God had stirred its waters would be healed. This poor old guy had been trying to make it for thirty-eight years without luck (or anyone to get him over and in) so Jesus came to his rescue: Jesus, who in chapter four, at Jacob's well in Shechem, had told the woman, "The water I give shall become a fountain within, leaping up to provide eternal life."

In a good-news-bad-news scene, the one-time cripple then cripples Jesus by identifying him to the authorities, who begin to persecute him for disrespecting the Sabbath prohibition on work (even on working miracles!).

Wednesday Fourth Week

Scripture

Isaiah 49: 8-15 *Thus says the Lord: In a time of favor I answer you, on the day of salvation I help you. / They shall not hunger or thirst, nor shall the sun strike them, / for he who pities them leads them, and guides them beside springs of water. / I will cut a road through all my mountains, and make my highways level. / Zion said, "The Lord has forsaken me; my Lord has forgotten me." / Can a mother forget her infant? / Even should she forget, I will never forget you.*

Responsorial Psalm 145: 8-9, 13-14, 17-18

John 5: 17-30 *The reason the Jews were even more determined to kill him was that he not only was breaking the Sabbath, but, worse still, was speaking of God as his own Father, thereby making himself God's equal. This was Jesus' answer: "The Son can do only what he sees the Father doing. Whatever the Father does, the Son does likewise. He who refuses to honor the Son refuses to honor the Father who sent him. The man who hears my word and has faith in him who sent me possesses eternal life.*

Reflection:
God is always watching over us, especially in our difficulties. Even to the extent of doing our job for us. Remember Isaiah 40 from the alternate first reading for the feast of the Baptism of the Lord? We are to lower the

hills and raise up the valleys, to make a country road into a freeway to enable an easy arrival for our visiting Lord. Here God commits himself, "I will cut a road through my mountains, and make my highways level… for the Lord comforts his people and shows mercy to his afflicted." Then, that unforgettably strong but tender guarantee: even should things get so bad that a mother might forget about her child in the process of saving herself, even then our God will never forget us.

The plot thickens, as they say. The Pharisees find it increasingly difficult to put up with Jesus, who not only disregards their laws, but now goes around identifying himself with Yahweh to the extreme of calling him his Father! This is blasphemy! Jesus calmly expounds: "The Father loves the Son, and everything the Father does he shows him. Yes, to your great wonderment, he will show him even greater works than these. He who refuses to honor the Son refuses to honor the Father who sent him." "The Father has assigned all judgment to the Son…and my judgment is honest, because I am not seeking my own will but the will of him who sent me."

What a gift we have in the Spirit's indwelling: we can believe our unbelievable closeness to God, the once-distant Transcendent One, in the humanity of our brother Jesus, one like us in all things but sin. No wonder one of the earliest heresies we had to clear up was the notion that Jesus, as God's Son, the second person of the Blessed Trinity, could not possibly be truly human (thus, unfortunately, not really one with us, one of us).

Thursday Fourth Week

Scripture

Exodus 32: 7-14 Moses has been up on Mount Sinai with God, when the Lord says to him, "You'd better get back to your people, whom you brought out from the land of Egypt: they've gone crazy! They've made themselves a molten calf and are dancing around, worshiping it, saying,

'This is your God, O Israel, who brought you out of the land of Egypt!' Let my wrath consume them. I'm going to wipe them out and start over. Then I will make of you a great nation." But Moses implored the Lord: "Why get so angry with your people, whom you brought out of the land of Egypt? Why should the Egyptians say, 'He brought them out into the desert, all right, but just so he could get rid of them'? Remember your servants Abraham, Isaac and Israel, and how you swore by your very self, 'All this land that I promised, I will give your descendants as their perpetual heritage.'" So the Lord relented.

Responsorial Psalm 106: 19-20, 21-22, 23 is a detailed depiction of the same event.

John 5: 31-47 Jesus said to the Jews: "If I were witnessing on my own behalf, you couldn't verify my testimony; but there is also someone else testifying on my behalf, John, who has testified to the truth. Why, the very works I perform testify on my behalf that the Father has sent me and is giving testimony on my behalf. The Scriptures in which you think you have eternal life—even they testify on my behalf. Don't think that I will be your accuser before the Father; the one who'll accuse you is the very Moses on whom you have set your hopes. If you believed Moses you would then believe me, because he was talking about me when he wrote."

Reflection:
In today's "Moses Mass" we see why he was held in the highest esteem, after Abraham. He was the people's Public Defender Number One. God was righteous (and right) in his reaction to the incredible insult they tossed his way when they credited the work of their own hands, the molten calf, with their rescue from Egypt. But Moses talked him down with a gentle but firm reminder that God had committed himself to his people's protection and eventual success. And instead of thanks, he gets continual grumbling and foot-dragging from the very people he has pulled out of the fire! By the way, did you notice the cute back-and-forth about whose idea it was in the first place? "Mo, get back to your people

whom you brought out." "Okay. But don't get so angry with your people whom you brought out."

Jesus is having a hard time with the same people for the same reason. They don't appreciate his role of mediator between a sinless God and a sinful humanity. They won't listen, because he doesn't fit their idea of a heaven-sent Messiah. For openers, he's not even one of them, trained in the law (with all its tricky little but-if-you-swear-by-the-gift-on-the-altar maneuvers).… For another, he calls the darnedest things a sin: just leering at a woman, just calling your brother a jerk in your heart.… Don't you love how he uses their "We're cool, we belong to Moses" to turn the tables on them? "You can't believe me, because you really don't believe Moses, and don't worry, you'll be hearing from <u>him</u> later."

Friday Fourth Week

Scripture

Wisdom 2: 1, 12-22 The wicked said, "Let's keep an eye on this goody-two-shoes; isn't he obnoxious? Just to see him is a pain, because he won't behave like normal folks. He keeps his distance from us, as if we were unclean or something, and he claims to be so close to God. Let's see what'll happen to him. If he is God's favorite, God will deliver him from persecution. Let's condemn him to a shameful death, since according to his own words, God will take care of him." That's what they thought, but they were mistaken; their wickedness blinded them, and they didn't count on God rewarding the holiness of an innocent soul.

Responsorial Psalm 34: 17-18, 19-20, 21, 23 *When the just cry out, the Lord hears them, and from all their distress he rescues them. The Lord is close to the brokenhearted; many are the troubles of the just man, but out of them all the Lord delivers him. He watches over all his bones, not one of them shall be broken.*

John 7: 1-2, 10, 25-30 Jesus had decided not to travel in Judea because some of the Jews were looking for a chance to kill him. When the feast of Booths drew near he went to Jerusalem, but in secret. Some of the people who saw him wondered, "Isn't this the one they want to kill? Here he is speaking in public and they don't say a word to him! Maybe even the authorities have decided that this is the Messiah. Still, we know where he comes from. When the Messiah comes, no one is supposed to know his origins." Jesus, teaching in the temple area, was irked: "So you know my origins? Fact is, I haven't come of myself. I was sent by the One who has the right to send, and him you don't know." At this, they tried to lay hands on him, but couldn't manage to lay a finger on him, because it wasn't his time to die yet.

Reflection:
Jesus feels the heat, but still goes to the Temple to teach his followers. Others are surprised: aren't the authorities supposed to be looking to silence this man? Maybe he has convinced them. Still, he can't fool us, because we have him figured out. Jesus bristles: "Oh, so you know me? Well, you don't know the One who sent me, because you still refuse to accept the good news that I bring you from him."

Both the first reading and Psalm 34 speak sadly of the sinful world's opposition to the good messenger from God. The Wisdom selection is almost spooky, it's so dead-on. It's hard to believe that this was written some 200 years before Christ. But, that's human nature for you—it's the same now as it was and will be, world without end. And the psalmist describes aptly the troubled, broken heart of one who reaches out in God's name and meets only resentment and resistance, even as he is guaranteed an eventual rescue.

Saturday Fourth Week

Scripture

Jeremiah 11: 18-20 *I, like a trusting lamb led to slaughter, had not realized that they were hatching plots against me. But you, Lord, searcher of mind and heart, let me witness the vengeance you take on them, for to you I have entrusted my cause.*

Responsorial Psalm 7: 2-3, 9-10, 11-12 *O Lord, in you I take refuge, save me from all my pursuers. Do me justice, O Lord, because of the innocence that is mine.*

John 7: 40-53 Some people, after hearing Jesus speak, began to say, "This must be the Prophet." Others claimed, "He is the Messiah." But some objected, "Doesn't Scripture say the Messiah, being of David's family, has to come from Bethlehem?" The crowd was quite confused about him. When the Temple guards returned, the chief priests and Pharisees asked them, "Why didn't you bring him in?" "We never heard anybody speak like that before." "Don't tell us he's fooled you too! You don't see any of us believing in him, do you? Only these idiots, who know nothing about the law—and they don't count anyway!" But then one of their own, Nicodemus (the one who had come to Jesus by night) said: "Since when does our law condemn any man without first hearing him and knowing the facts?" "Don't tell us you're a Galilean too," they taunted him. "Look it up. You won't find the Prophet coming from Galilee."

Reflection:
The evangelist becomes a reporter with a mike, doing man-in the-street stories. The crowd had conflicting opinions about Jesus. What a hang-up these Judeans had about the people from the north, these Galilean outsiders. "There's no way any of them would have anything to teach us." And then there's the Pharisees' hang-up about the unwashed (literally) masses, their own countrymen, whose opinion counts for nothing, since they

know nothing about the law. When one of them objects,"Speaking of the law, since when is it okay to condemn someone without giving him a chance to explain himself?" their answer is strictly ad hominem: "Don't tell us you're one of them?" They're running scared, pure and simple, and Jesus is now in big trouble. Hang on, Good Friday's coming in under two weeks.

Jeremiah is being unjustly persecuted, and his only recourse is to turn to God, that just searcher of mind and heart, and ask for vindication. Not being quite the guy that Jesus is, he will also ask for front-row tickets to the come-uppance of his foes. (Is Jesus special, or what? "But I say to you, pray for those who persecute you.")

FEAST OF THE ANNUNCIATION (floater: March 25th)

Scripture

Isaiah 7:10-14 *The LORD spoke to Ahaz: Ask for a sign from the LORD. But Ahaz answered, "I will not ask! I will not tempt the LORD!" Then he said: Listen, the Lord himself will give you this sign: the virgin shall be with child, and bear a son, and shall name him Emmanuel.*

Hebrews 10: 5-10 *First he says, "Sacrifices and offerings, holocausts and sin offerings, you neither desired nor delighted in." These are offered according to the law. Then he says, "Behold, I come to do your will." He takes away the first to establish the second. By this "will," we have been consecrated through the offering of the body of Jesus Christ once for all.*

Luke 1:26-38 *In the sixth month, the angel Gabriel was sent from God to a virgin betrothed to a man named Joseph. Coming to her, he said, "Hail, favored one! The Lord is with you. You have found favor with God. Behold, you will conceive in your womb and bear a son, and you shall name him Jesus." Mary said to the angel, "How can this be, since*

I have no relations with a man?" And the angel said, "The holy Spirit will come upon you, and the power of the Most High will overshadow you." Mary said, "Behold, I am the handmaid of the Lord. May it be done to me according to your word."

Reflection:

Isaiah reports God's frustration at the outwardly submissive King Ahaz, whose reluctance to ask for a sign ("I will not tempt the Lord") masks the fact that he has already, on his own, sought protection for his kingdom from an alliance with other (pagan) kings. Can you imagine: ruling in Yahweh's name and not trusting in God to come to his aid but instead turning to pagans for help?

So Isaiah relays God's glorious promised sign: "the virgin [in Hebrew almah, a young girl and therefore virginal] shall...bear a son, and shall name him Emmanuel," which means God-is-with-us. In the later, Spirit-filled understanding of the Apostles, Mary's virginity was not seen as an automatic reflection of her youth, but as reflecting her choice to remain totally faithful to God's wonderful call to the motherhood of his Son. (What the Church would render in the Latin virgo rather than the Hebrew almah.)

Mary's question to the angel contains none of the intransigence of Ahaz's objection to Isaiah. She simply wonders how God will bring about her pregnancy, since she has no man in her future. Learning that God will take care of this himself, through the power of the Holy Spirit, she graciously submits to his plan.

Placed between the promise of a king of peace and the joy of the Annunciation, this passage from the Letter to the Hebrews is a sobering reminder that the crib is never far from the cross. Our thoughts go from Christmas to Calvary, because we know Jesus took on our human existence so that he could lift it from slavery to sin into the freedom of God's own life. The author was particularly interested in Temple rituals and the value of sacrificial offerings in gaining us God's favor. The old offerings were seen as cleansing and consecrating the people to God. Jesus' sacrificial death does so "once for all," no need for any more ritual killing of animals ever again, since Christ destroys the power of sin over us by putting our sins to death on his cross. This is how our Messiah will save us: not by military victories, but by taking on our defeats and becoming a "loser" to make winners out of us!

Fifth Sunday of Lent

Cycle A – Scripture

Ezekiel 37: 12-14 *Thus says the Lord God: O my people, I will open your graves and have you rise from them and bring you back to the land of Israel. I will put my spirit in you that you may live and know that I am the Lord. I have promised, and I will do it, says the Lord.*

Responsorial Psalm 130: 1-2, 3-4, 5-6, 7-8 *Out of the depths I cry to you, Lord.*

Romans 8: 8-11 *If Christ is in you, the body is dead because of sin, while the spirit lives because of justice. If the Spirit of him who raised Jesus from the dead dwells in you, then he who raised Christ from the dead will bring your mortal bodies to life also through his Spirit dwelling in you.*

John 11: 1-45 (shorter 11: 3-7, 17, 20-27, 33-45) In Bethany lived the two sisters, Mary and Martha, and their brother Lazarus; they sent word to Jesus when Lazarus fell ill. But Jesus said, *"This sickness is not to end in death; rather it is for God's glory, that through it the Son of God may be glorified."* After waiting two days he told his disciples they were going back to Judea, *"Our beloved Lazarus has fallen asleep, but I am going there to wake him."* The disciples wondered why all the fuss, because they thought he meant sleep in the sense of slumber. But Jesus told them plainly: Lazarus is dead. For your sakes I am glad I was not there, that you may come to believe. Lazarus had already been in the tomb four days when Jesus finally arrived. Martha heard he was coming, and went to meet him, *"Lord, if you had been here, my brother would never have died."* She hints that even now God would answer Jesus' prayer for her brother. He assures her that her brother will rise again. She says, I know, in the resurrection at the last day. Jesus tells her: *"I am the resurrection and the life; whoever believes in me, though he should die, will come to life; and whoever is alive and believes in me will never die."* Soon Mary has the same conversation with him. Jesus is overcome with emotion and asks to be taken to the tomb. He orders the stone be moved away and looking up, prays: *"Father, I thank you for having heard me. I know that you always hear me, but I have said this for the sake of the crowd, that they may believe that you sent me. Then he called loudly: Lazarus, come out!"* The ensuing miracle causes many of those who had come to comfort the sisters to put their faith in Jesus.

Reflection:
Ezekiel's vision depicts dramatically God's saving power. In a field full of sun-bleached, scattered bones, he witnesses the result of God's call back to life. The bones will rustle together into skeletons, some flesh gets slapped on them, and pretty soon it's like nothing happened—the dead have come back to life! God's mercy will do this. It can revive us way after we have given up hope. We have his promise on it. Paul relays the same hopeful message to the Christians in Rome. Even though the body is dead because of sin, the Spirit ("breath of life") that brought Jesus back to life now dwells in us, and will bring our mortal bodies back to life also.

In the story of the raising of Lazarus, we see enacted the promised rescue from our death in sin. All seems lost. It's too late to hope for a miracle. Hold it! What do you mean it's too late? God can reach into our graves and put us back together; his Spirit can be breathed back into lifeless lungs to start a new heartbeat...and Jesus represents both the Father and the Spirit at work when he calls Lazarus back out into the land of the living, the life of grace.

Fifth Sunday of Lent

Cycle B – Scripture

Jeremiah 31: 31-34 *The days are coming, says the Lord, when I will make a new covenant with the house of Israel and the house of Judah. I will place my law within them, and write it upon their hearts; I will be their God and they shall be my people. No longer will they have need to teach [anyone] how to know the Lord. All, from least to greatest, shall know me, says the Lord, for I will forgive their evildoing and remember their sin no more.*

Responsorial Psalm 51: 3-4, 12-13, 14-15

Hebrews 5: 7-9 *Son though he was, he learned obedience from what he suffered; and when perfected, he became the source of eternal salvation for all who obey him.*

John 12: 20-33 *Unless the grain of wheat falls to the earth and dies, it remains just a grain of wheat. But if it dies, it produces much fruit. My soul is troubled now, yet what should I say—Father, save me from this hour? But it was for this that I came to this hour. Father, glorify your name! Now has judgment come upon this world, now will this world's prince be driven out, and I—once I am lifted up from earth—will draw all men to myself. (This statement of his indicated the sort of death he was going to die.)*

Reflection:

Yahweh's faithful love impels him to erase our sins and make possible a new beginning for us. This time, he says, it's going to work, because he's got a new, improved plan of attack. No more stone tablets for us to read! He's going to write his law upon our hearts, so we won't have to go look them up or ask anybody about them again. He will place his law within us, so we won't need to be taught about it any more. We'll be walking, talking Decalogs! What a God! He had been desperately hoping to find faithful followers who wouldn't stray, and now he has found a way: he will implant his own little GPS in their hearts! [Come, Holy Spirit, fill the hearts of your faithful!]

My dad would tell me about a friend from his youth (Depression era in San Francisco) who could never afford to travel, yet every year would pick up brochures, maps, travel hints, etc., for his "vacation trip." He'd read about it, talk about it, daydream about it, imagine himself going through the sites pictured, etc. (imagine if they could google back then!), and then, once the ten days were up, "return" and get on with his regular life. Interesting, no? I have an idea Paul meant something like this when he claims that Jesus learned from what he suffered. The difference between "knowing" suffering and living it. Jesus came to experience our life, to share our hardships and limitations, and then teach us how to get through it all somehow. That's why we need to follow him, because he has gone through it himself, he knows the way…he is the way.

Jesus faces his impending death, and knows his life will be made productive by his death. What a beautiful truth in a grain of wheat! Notice how different from the Synoptics' is John's portrayal of Jesus in the Garden: no agonizing, not even a reluctance. Should I ask the Father to spare me? It was just for this confrontation that I came. Bring it on! I came to give life to the world—my life, if need be—and this is where it starts.

Fifth Sunday of Lent

Cycle C – Scripture

Isaiah 43: 16-21 *Thus says the Lord, Remember not the past; see, I am doing something new! Do you not perceive it? In the desert I make a way, in the wasteland, rivers, for my chosen people to drink.*

Responsorial Psalm 126: 1-2, 2-3, 4-5, 5 *When the Lord brought back the captives of Zion, we were like men dreaming, then [we] were filled with rejoicing. The Lord has done great things for us; we are glad indeed. Although they go forth weeping, carrying the seed to be sown, they shall come back rejoicing, carrying their sheaves.*

Philippians 3: 6-14 *I have accounted all else rubbish so that Christ may be my wealth and I may be in him, not having any justice of my own based on observance of the law. The justice I possess is that which comes through faith in Christ. Thus do I hope that I may arrive at resurrection from the dead.*

John 8: 1-11 As Jesus was teaching in the Temple area the scribes and Pharisees brought a woman forward who had been caught in adultery and made her stand there in front of everyone. *"Teacher, in the law Moses ordered such women to be stoned. What do you have to say about the case?"* *(They were posing this question to trap him, so that they could have something to accuse him of.)* Jesus didn't answer, just bent down and started writing in the dirt with his finger. When they persisted, he straightened up and proposed, "Let the man among you who has no sin be the first to cast a stone at her," and went back to his writing. Then they drifted away one by one, beginning with the elders.

Reflection:

Nobody knows what it was that Jesus wrote on the ground, but it's okay to wonder: was it "it takes two to tango, where's the dude?" Or could he have been writing down her johns' license plate numbers—some of them disturbingly familiar? Maybe he was listing some sins to alert anybody who might be tempted to be the first to cast a stone. Whatever. The point is that the Pharisees cared nothing about the woman, it was all a set-up. But Christ saw in her a sister, not an object, and treated her gently, even as he dismissed her with a clear warning, "From now on, avoid this sin." This is Jesus our Savior, our gentle judge: in our defense, he will not hesitate to make enemies, even powerful ones. We'll soon see where this leads him.

Paul knows that observance of the law does not justify him. Only faith in Christ's love for him assures him of salvation. And that love is impressive, drawing him to share in the suffering and death of Christ, in hope of arriving with Christ at the resurrection from the dead. So this world has nothing to offer Paul. His whole attention is on his life on high in Christ Jesus.

This passage from Isaiah dates from the Babylonian Captivity. Certainly God had worked wonders in the Exodus, bringing them out of Egyptian slavery some seven centuries earlier (cf. Psalm 126). Now God is working new wonders for his people, who find themselves once again helpless captives in need of being freed. God leads them, through their new Exodus, back home. And Jesus, our new Moses, will lead us on our true Exodus, not from Egypt or Babylon to a promised land, but from this earthly, sinful existence to our true home in heaven, just what Paul was talking about. If we stumble and fall, even if we choose to return to sin, as soon as we ask for help, there he is to extend a helping hand. He is our judge, but he's also our mighty Savior. The fact that he must pay a price to save us, that he must die so we may live, does not deter him. Let us pray that we might all love, and serve, in the same saving way.

OPTIONAL MASS for any weekday of the Fifth Week of Lent, especially on the years of a B or C Cycle. On a Cycle A year, the gospel is used on the Fifth Sunday of Lent.

Scripture

2 Kings 4:18-21, 32-37 A generous Shunammite couple has arranged for the prophet Elisha to lodge with them. Tragically, their young son dies. The mother shows her faith by leaving his lifeless body on the prophet's bed. When he discovers him, he stretches his body over the young boy's and prays. The body becomes warm. On the second time, the boy sneezes seven times and opens his eyes, and Elisha returns him alive to his mother.

Responsorial Psalm 17:1, 6-7, 8, 15
John 11:1-45 We've seen the story of the raising of Lazarus on the Fifth Sunday of Lent, p. 71.

Reflection:
These two resurrection accounts taught the catechumens the power of Jesus, how he could raise them back to life from the death of their sinful past by their upcoming bath in the baptismal waters.

Monday Fifth Week

Scripture

Daniel 13: 1-9, 15-17, 19-30, 33-62 A man named Joakim lived in Babylon, married to a very beautiful and God-fearing woman, Susanna. Two elders of the people had been appointed judges (the kind the Lord had warned about, *"Wickedness has come out of Babylon: from the elders who were to govern the people as judges"*). They watched Susanna take her daily walk in the garden, and they began to lust for her. One day, when she decided to bathe, they saw their chance. She sent her maids to the house for her soap and oils. Nobody else was there except the two elders, who had hidden themselves and were watching her. As soon as the maids had left, the two [dirty] old men [I'm sorry, I couldn't stop myself] hurried to her and said, "Lie with us. If you refuse, we will testify that you dismissed your maids because you had a young man hidden here."

"I'm trapped," she realized. "If I refuse, I cannot escape your power. Yet it is better for me to fall into your power without guilt than to sin before the Lord." So she screamed for help, and the old men also shouted.

When the people in the house heard them they rushed to the garden to see what had happened. The judges claimed the young man had gotten away because he was too young and strong for them. He next day, the two wicked elders came, determined to put Susanna to death. All her relatives and the onlookers were weeping; nothing like this had ever been said about her before. The assembly felt obligated to agree with the elders—it was two against one—so they condemned her to death.

Susanna prayed aloud: "O eternal God, you know they have testified falsely against me. Here I am about to die, though I have done nothing wrong." The Lord heard her prayer. And as she was being led to execution, he stirred up the spirit of a young man named Daniel, who cried aloud: "Are you such fools, O Israelites, to condemn a woman of Israel without further examination? Return to court, for they have testified falsely against her." He told them to separate the two judges and bring them in one by one. He called the first: "How you have grown evil with age! Tell me under what tree you saw them together." "Under a mastic tree." Putting him to one side he ordered the other one to be brought, [and he said] "under an oak."

The whole assembly cried aloud, blessing God for saving all who put their hope in him. They rose up against the two elders and, in accord with the law of Moses, inflicted on them the penalty they had plotted to impose on her, and put them to death. Hooray for Yahweh!

Responsorial Psalm 23: 1-3, 3-4, 5, 6

[In cycles "A" and "B" today's Gospel is John 8:1-11 (the woman taken in adultery, please consult p. 75.) In cycle "C" that was yesterday's Sunday Gospel, so today we use the following.]

John 8: 12-20 *Jesus said to the Jews, "I am the light of the world. No follower of mine shall ever walk in darkness, he shall possess the light of life." The Pharisees [said], "You are your own witness. Such testimony cannot be valid." Jesus answered, "I am not alone; I have at my side the*

One who sent me, the Father. In your law evidence given by two persons is valid. I am one of those testifying in my behalf, the Father who sent me is the other." "And where is this Father of yours?" "You know neither me nor my Father. If you knew me, you would know my Father too." He went unapprehended, because his hour had not yet come.

Reflection:

God works through the smarts of a young man He stirs up to question the integrity of the two wicked judges. And the kid does not miss his chance to glorify his own people. "This is how you acted with the daughters of Israel [the northern tribes] and in their fear they yielded to you. But a daughter of Judah [you go, girl] did not tolerate your wickedness." The trust Susanna placed in God was not misplaced. When she was trapped, and all seemed lost, she remained loyal to God, and he remained loyal to her. Good lesson.

The conflict between Jesus and the Pharisees escalates and becomes nasty. He minces no words with them, flat out accusing them of not knowing their God, his Father. He still remains at large, but only because it was not yet time for him to fall into their hands.

Tuesday Fifth Week

Scripture

Numbers 21: 4-9 *The people complained against God and Moses [and] in punishment saraph serpents bit [them] so that many of them died. [They] said, "We have sinned in complaining against the Lord and you. Pray the Lord to take the serpents from us." So the Lord said to Moses, "Make a saraph and mount it on a pole, and if anyone who has been bitten looks at it, he will recover."*

Responsorial Psalm 102: 2-3, 16-18, 19-21

John 8: 21-30 *Jesus said to the Pharisees: "You belong to what is below; I belong to what is above. You belong to this world—a world that cannot hold me. When you lift up the Son of Man, you will realize that I AM and that I do nothing by myself. I say only what the Father has taught me. The One who sent me is with me. He has not deserted me, hence I always do what pleases him." Because he spoke this way, many came to believe in him.*

Reflection:
The word "seraph" means "fiery" and refers to the effect of the bite of this venomous snake. (More on this later.) The people quickly put one and one together and beg Moses to work on God while they work on shutting up. God's curious prescription is not explained, but it works, so that's good enough. Ever wonder why the medical profession is symbolized by the snake(s) entwined around a stick? In the early Church, we shall see Jesus on the cross as the sign of our healing from the wounds of sin.

The unexplained reference to the lifting up of the Son of Man has always been read as a hint of his coming crucifixion. And for Jewish converts, the salutary effects of their Savior's crucifixion, his being lifted up on the cross, meant their return from the death of sin and alienation from God to a new life with God. "You will surely die in your sins unless you come to believe that I AM"—an unmistakable claim to oneness with the Father for Jesus, and for all those who follow him through suffering/death to his risen life once more with the Father.

It's interesting that there's no report (in John's depiction of Jesus' death) of the desolate cry: "Why have you forsaken me?" quoted from Psalm 22. The Jesus of John's Gospel is so closely identified with his Father that he never feels that the Father has left him, even in his most difficult situations. This is the strength that allows Jesus at the Garden, for example, to not agonize (as portrayed by other evangelists) but to simply say, "Now my soul is troubled. What shall I say: Father, save me from this hour? It was for this very reason that I have come to this hour!" (John 12:27). Bring it on!

[P.S. Now comes your penance for reading something written by a Franciscan. The word "seraph" (burning, ardent) appears also as the name of that loving choir of angels. Remember the seraphim? St. Francis of Assisi was recognized as being so moved by his burning love for Jesus that he is known as the "Seraphic" founder of the Seraphic Order, the Franciscans!]

[P.P.S. Please pray for us, so it won't remain a label, but become a reality. Thanks.]

Wednesday Fifth Week

Scripture

Daniel 3: 14-29, 91-92, 95 If the three young Jews defy the royal order to worship Nebuchadnezzar's favorite idol they must be cast into the white-hot furnace, "*and who is the God that can deliver you out of my hands?*" Shadrach, Meshach and Abednego answered the king, "If our God can save us from the furnace, and from your hands, O King, may He save us! But even if he chooses not to, we will not worship the golden statue you set up." Nebuchadnezzar, livid with rage, ordered the furnace to be heated seven times more than usual and Shadrach, Meshach and Abednego [bound] and cast into the white-hot furnace. Afterwards, he asked his nobles, "Didn't we cast three men, bound, into the fire? I can see four, unfettered and unhurt, walking in the fire, and the fourth looks like a son of God." Then, when he catches on, he says, "Blessed be their God who sent his angel to deliver his servants who trusted in him; they disobeyed my royal command and gave up their bodies rather than serve or worship any god except their own God." Hooray for Yahweh, again!

Responsorial Psalm: Daniel 3: 52 – 56 (the praises they sang to God from the fiery pit)

John 8: 33-42 *Jesus said to those Jews who believed in him: "If you live according to my teaching, you are truly my disciples; then you will know the truth, and the truth will set you free." "We are descendants of Abraham," was their answer. "Never have we been slaves to anyone." Jesus answered: "Every one who lives in sin is the slave of sin. If the son frees you, you will really be free. I realize you are of Abraham's stock. Nevertheless, you are trying to kill me because my word finds no hearing among you."*

Reflection:

A beautiful story of the brave loyalty of these Jewish boys, known also by their Hebrew names: Azariah, Hananiah, and Mishael. I love the "seven times more than usual"—I guess that shows the king was really ticked. To his credit, however, he cools right down and praises the God who obviously has delivered his loyal followers because of their impressive trust. The praises they sing to God are not to be missed. Please make a point of looking up Daniel 3: 52-90. (Verse 66 might have been tough to get out, but 67-70 must have been fun!) I bet you'll enjoy praying them as well.

In this Gospel's verbal scrimmaging, Jesus makes it clear he knows what he's up against, "you are trying to kill me." It doesn't come any clearer than that. And yet, there's no stopping him. He continues his efforts to reach them, to open their eyes, to unstop their ears, to reach their hearts…even as his own heart is breaking with the sorrow of their rejection. How about us? Are we making it difficult for Christ to reach us, or are we opening our lives to his call, are we getting ourselves out of the way and making more room for him to live in us and through us? Are we using this penitential season to change, or just putting in time till Easter?

Wednesday Fifth Week

Scripture

Genesis 17: 3-9 *God spoke to [Abram], "My covenant with you is this: your name shall be Abraham, for I am making you the father of a host of nations. I will maintain my covenant with you and your descendants after you throughout the ages in an everlasting pact to be your God and [theirs]. On your part, you and your descendants must keep my covenant throughout the ages."*

Responsorial Psalm 105: 4-5, 6-7, 8-9 recalls that wondrous event.

John 8: 51-59 *Jesus said: "If a man is true to my word he shall never see death." "Now we know you are possessed," the Jews retorted. "Abraham is dead. Surely you do not pretend to be greater than our father Abraham, who died!" Jesus answered, "Your father Abraham rejoiced that he might see my day. He saw it and was glad." The Jews objected: "You are not yet fifty! How can you have seen Abraham?" Jesus answered, "Before Abraham came to be, I AM." At that they picked up rocks to throw at Jesus, but he hid himself and slipped out of the temple precincts.*

Reflection:

In this "Abraham Mass" we revisit God's offer of covenant friendship for all ages. And speaking of ages, when Jesus claims he dealt with Abraham, the Jews ridicule him: "You're still in your prime. How could you have seen him?" But Jesus is serious—he is making a sober and solemn statement; he does not back off. So, either he's crazy (possessed) or he's seriously claiming oneness with their Yahweh, the great I AM, and deserves to be stoned to death for this unthinkable blasphemy.

No other evangelist works so hard—or so clearly—at establishing this oneness of Yahweh and Jesus. Remember the contrast between their bios of Jesus? Mark won't waste time establishing Jesus' credentials—he'll start writing when Jesus starts working. Matthew begins with Abraham, Luke goes back all the way to Adam. But John places Jesus beyond time, before it all started, sharing God's awesome pre-existence to us and to everything else that is.

That's why the Passion is so shattering. We can hardly believe that "God so loved the world that he gave his only Son, so that everyone who believes in him might not perish but might have eternal life" (that famous 3: 16). Isn't this the God who stopped Abraham's knife in mid-air and told him he was just testing him—he didn't really have to return his only son's life, his demonstrated willingness proved his complete loyalty? And now the Father is asking his Son to go to whatever lengths it takes to show us how much they both love us! What love the Father has for us! What love his Son shows us! What love the Spirit fills us with! And what are we doing with all that love?

Friday Fifth Week

Scripture

Jeremiah 20: 10-13 *The Lord is with me, like a mighty champion; my persecutors will stumble, they will not triumph. O Lord, to you I have entrusted my cause. Praise the Lord, for he has rescued the life of the poor from the power of the wicked!*

Responsorial Psalm 18: 2-3, 3-4, 5-6, 7

John 10: 31-42 *When the Jews reached for rocks to stone him, Jesus protested: "Many good deeds have I shown you from the Father. For which of these do you stone me?" "It is not for any 'good deed' that we are stoning you, but for blaspheming. You who are only a man are making yourself God." Jesus answered, "If I do not perform my Father's* *works, put no faith in me. But if I do perform them, even though you put no faith in me, put faith in these works, [and] realize what it means that the Father is in me and I in him."*

Reflection:

Jeremiah hears the whispers, he is aware of the plot on his life. But he trusts in the Lord's power to rescue him. (The responsorial psalm echoes his cry and his confidence.) He will not cease to bring his hostile audience the message God has entrusted to him.

Jesus likewise is busy doing the works his Father has charged him to carry out. But all he gets for his pains is a growing, menacing rejection. His problem? They got his message–they just can't understand it. How can a man claim so great an intimacy with God?

You can hardly blame them. It is unbelievable, from a human, logical perspective, that God calls us sinners so close to himself, that he showers his grace and his holiness on us even when we are still in sin. But that's the Good News! God loves us so much that he makes his sinless Son to be sin, so that we sinners can become the very holiness of God! Jesus has redeemed us—at a great price! How can we be so meager in our return of love to God when we consider his uncontainable lavishing of love on us?

Saturday Fifth Week

Scripture

Ezekiel 37: 21-28 *Thus speaks the Lord God: I will make [the Israelites] one nation. Never again will they be divided into two kingdoms. No longer shall they defile themselves with their idols. I will deliver them from all their sins, so that they may be my people and I may be their God.*

I will make with them a covenant of peace; it shall be everlasting.
I will be their God and they shall be my people. My sanctuary shall be
set up among them forever.

Responsorial Psalm: Jeremiah 31: 10, 11-12, 13 *He who scattered Israel,*
now gathers them together; he guards them as a shepherd his flock.

John 11: 45-57 *The chief priests and the Pharisees called a meeting of*
the Sanhedrin. "What are we to do with this man? If we let him go on like
this, the whole world will believe him. Then the Romans will come and
sweep away our sanctuary and our nation." Caiaphas, the high priest,
[said] "It is better to have one man die than to have the whole nation
destroyed." From that day onward there was a plan to kill [Jesus]. The
Jewish Passover was near, [and] they were on the lookout for Jesus.

Reflection:
You can feel the excitement in Ezekiel's words—they spill out in enthusiastic repetition. This reform, this purification, this new beginning that
will last for all time, this gathering of all his people under one prince: it's
the Good News of the New Covenant. And Jesus on the cross will be the
covenant offering, traditionally sacrificed and split open, that will seal
this wonderful new pact for all people, for all time.

Faced with the challenge of Jesus gaining a popular following, and thus,
presumably, provoking a tightening of Roman control over their province
(and consequently a loss of their own power), the authorities opt for a
simple solution: get rid of the problem by killing one man and avoiding
a bloodbath for the entire nation. Simple. So Jesus' fate is settled.

Jesus knew what was coming. He felt it every time he tried in vain to
make his case to the powers-that-be. They felt it every time he spoke, so
clearly did his words indict them. But he kept speaking, trying so hard to
have them hear his Father's message, regardless of the danger to himself.
He was on a mission—to save us. Think where it will take him, and why.

INTRODUCTION TO HOLY WEEK

"Jesus suffers for us! He pays a price for us. He is victim. He shares the physical evils of man to cure him from moral evil, to cancel in Himself our sins. Sorrow which in the natural world is an isolated thing, for Jesus is a point of encounter, a communion…. You may lack all things, but not Jesus on the Cross. He is with you. He is with you." Pope Paul VI, quoted in the Vatican II Sunday Missal.

Interesting that the first and fundamental of the Buddha's insightful Four Noble Truths is "Suffering is universal." We may not all enjoy good health, or wealth, or power, but we certainly all share the experience of pain, of lack, of privation. This is where Jesus comes to meet us, to gather all humanity with him and take us not simply out of our suffering, but through it with him to glory.

Palm Sunday

Scripture

Gospel commemorating the Lord's entry into Jerusalem:

Cycle A

Matthew 21: 1-11 Coming close to Jerusalem, Jesus sent two disciples ahead to find and bring him an ass tethered with her colt beside her. *This came about to fulfill what was said through the prophet: "Tell the daughter of Zion: Your king comes to you without display, astride an ass, astride a colt, the foal of a beast of burden."* They did so, and when he mounted, the huge crowd began spreading their cloaks on the road before him, and others cut branches from trees to lay in his path. They were all crying out: *God save the Son of David! Blessed be he who comes in the name of the Lord! God save him from on high!* The whole town was asking "Who is this?" And the crowd would answer, "This is the prophet Jesus from Nazareth in Galilee."

Reflection:
Zechariah 9:9 had prophesied just such an entry for the Messiah into his city (David's descendant—David's city). In fact, it was David who went out on an ass when Samuel gathered his followers and anointed him as Saul's successor by Yahweh's designated Plan B for the one to rule his people in his name. The humble beast of burden speaks of David's lowly beginnings as a shepherd, but also reminds all of his God-given task of shepherding God's people. Remember Jesus explaining to his apostles, "You know that among the pagans the rulers lord it over them, and their great men make their authority felt. This is not to happen among you. No; anyone who wants to be great among you must be your servant, just as the Son of Man came not to be served but to serve" (Matthew 20: 25-28). Ergo, a SHEPHERD-king, meek, on an ass.

Cycle B

Mark 11: 1-10 Coming close to Jerusalem, Jesus dispatches two disciples to enter town and fetch him a colt, as yet unridden, that they will find there. If asked, they are to say that the Master needs it. It happened just that way. They bring it to Jesus, lay their cloaks on it for him to ride, spread their cloaks on the road ahead, while others spread reeds they had cut in the fields. They all cried out: *Hosannah! Blessed be he who comes in the name of the Lord! Blessed be the reign of our father David to come! God save him from on high!*

Reflection:
Again, it is not the image of a worldly ruler astride a high-stepping steed. Instead, it is purposefully humble: the colt of an ass. And yet, the great-

est king in their history rode a donkey as his career began. The power is not the king's—it is Yahweh's.

OR alternate: John 12: 12-16 *The great crowd that had come for the feast heard that Jesus was to enter Jerusalem, so they got palm branches and came out to meet him, shouting: "Hosanna! Blessed is he who comes in the name of the Lord!" The disciples did not understand all this, but after Jesus was glorified they recalled that the people had done precisely what had been written.*

Reflection:
Jesus enters the city of David riding a donkey, fulfilling the prophecy of Zechariah 9: 9 "O daughter of Zion, your king approaches you on a donkey's colt," and recalling the Davidic tradition: "they mounted Solomon on King David's mule and anointed [him]" (1Kings 1: 38). Early kings humbly left the glory to God, in whose name they ruled. Horses (and chariots) were seen as symbols of the pagan kings' self-centered power.

Cycle C

Luke 19: 28-40 As they approach Jerusalem, Jesus sends ahead disciples who fill find an ass tied there which no one has yet ridden. Untie it and lead it back. Done. They spread their cloaks on the roadway, and on his approach to the descent from Mount Olivet, *the entire crowd of disciples began to rejoice and praise God loudly, "Blessed be he who comes as king in the name of the Lord! Peace in heaven and glory in the highest!" Some of the Pharisees in the crowd said to him, "Teacher, rebuke your disciples." He replied, "If they were to keep silence, I tell you the very stones would cry out."*

Reflection:
This is a courageous move on the part of Jesus, this public entry. Everybody knows the authorities are lined up against him and looking for any excuse to arrest him and bring him down. And yet, it is his destiny: if

my disciples were forced to keep silent, the very stones would cry out in their stead!

Scripture for the Mass

Cycle A – B – C

Isaiah 50: 4-7 *I gave my back to those who beat me, my cheeks to those who plucked my beard; my face I did not shield from buffets and spitting. The Lord God is my help, therefore I am not disgraced.*

Responsorial Psalm 22: 8-9, 17-18, 19-20, 23-24

Philippians 2: 6-11 *Though he was in the form of God [Christ] did not deem equality with God something to be grasped at. Rather, he emptied himself and took the form of a slave, obediently accepting even death, death on a cross!*

Reflection:

Among the famous four Songs of the Suffering Servant from Second Isaiah, this third one is shockingly descriptive of the Lord's sufferings leading up to his crucifixion. Jesus, like the Servant, is under vicious attack, but nonetheless rallies daily to speak for God, who has given him this mission. "I have not turned back." He stands up to beatings and ridicule, beard-pulling and spitting in his face. "I have set my face like flint, knowing that I shall not be put to shame."

This famous passage contains the <u>kenosis</u> concept (it means "emptying" in Greek) that describes the process Jesus undertook in order to come to us, give us the example of his life and death, and lead us home to our Father. He willingly accepted all the limitations of our human condition, so he could (from the inside!) overcome all its weaknesses (even death) and teach us how to do the same. His Father was so appreciative of the generosity Jesus showed, that, after his death, he restored to him all the glory he had left behind, and "bestowed on him the name above every other name, so that at Jesus' name, every knee must bend, and every tongue proclaim to the glory of God the Father: JESUS CHRIST IS LORD!"

Gospel Scripture

[It would be a sin to try to condense these, even worse to paraphrase them, so please give yourself the time to read the complete, or at least the shortened, version.]

Cycle A

Matthew 26: 13 – 27: 66 (shorter version 27: 11-54)
The Passion of our Lord Jesus Christ according to Matthew.

Reflection:
Matthew's account will consistently point out every detail that can be traced back to an Old Testament source, as he stresses how Jesus is the Messiah, the fulfillment all the Old Testament hints and longings and prophecies about the One God would send to save us. For the rest of it, his presentation is very little changed from his source—Mark—so please consult the Reflection following.

Cycle B

Mark 14: 1 – 15: 47 (shorter 15: 1-49)
The Passion of our Lord Jesus Christ according to Mark.

Reflection:
Mark is stark. From the moment he prays in the Garden—in agony over his impending death—Jesus falls to the ground (14:35), as opposed to kneeling in prayer, as depicted by Luke (22:41). His disciples fail him, one after the other. He asks them to pray with him, and three times (Luke will tell of only one instance) he returns to find them sleeping away instead of lending him support in his prayer. Judas betrays him. Peter (the Rock?) denies him with repeated curses. His followers are so quick to leave him that the last one leaves behind his clothes in the grasp of his questioners as he gets away naked—ironically the <u>opposite</u> of leaving all things to <u>follow him</u>. The only words we hear from Jesus on the cross are from psalm 22: "My God, my God, why have you forsaken me?"

Mark writes his gospel for a church that is facing, even undergoing, persecution. He wants his listeners to have the courage to choose death. So he presents Jesus in their same situation. In order to be faithful to his vocation, Jesus had to face death. Was it "easy" for him because he was God? Not the way Mark tells it. It was just as hard for him to accept death as it would be for them. The fact that their faith assured them that suffering and death lead to life didn't make it any easier to undergo their pain.

Cycle C

Luke 22: 14 – 23:56 (shorter 23: 1-49)
The Passion of our Lord Jesus Christ according to Luke.

Reflection:
Luke's Passion account presents disciples who are loyal: "you have stood by me in my trials," Jesus tells them (22: 28); whereas in Mark's Passion they all flee. During the agony in the garden, Luke's disciples are caught sleeping only once (three times in Matthew: "they could not keep their eyes open" 26:43) but it's because of their grief (22: 45). Jesus' anguish seems to come as much from the sufferings of others as from his own:

he heals the servant's ear (22:51); he consoles the grieving women of Jerusalem (23: 28-30). In spite of everything happening to him, he can't seem to stop thinking of others: he forgives his executioners (23: 34); he promises Paradise to the repentant thief dying beside him when he asks for a kind thought (23: 43). What a lovely and providential inclusion—he's the only evangelist to report that gory but beautiful, consoling encounter. And after all that, Jesus dies peacefully, praying "Father, into your hands I commend my spirit" with his final breath.

Monday of Holy Week

Scripture

Isaiah 42: 1-7 *Here is my servant whom I uphold, / my chosen one with whom I am pleased, / upon whom I have put my spirit. / I, the Lord, have grasped you by the hand; / I formed you, and set you / as a covenant of the people, / a light to the nations, / to open the eyes of the blind, / to bring out prisoners from confinement, / and from the dungeon, those who live in darkness.*

Responsorial Psalm 27: 1, 2, 3, 13-14

John 12: 1-11 A week before Passover Jesus came to Bethany, the village of Lazarus whom Jesus had raised from the dead. While he reclined at table, Mary brought costly perfume with which she anointed Jesus' feet, filling the whole house with its aroma. Then she dried his feet with her hair. Judas protested: "Why was this perfume not sold? The money could have been given to the poor." Jesus countered, "Leave her alone. Let her do it looking forward to the day they prepare me for burial." The chief priests planned to kill Lazarus too, because many Jews were going over to Jesus and believing in him on account of Lazarus.

Reflection:

This first of four descriptions of Isaiah's Suffering Servant fits Jesus like a glove: anointed with God's spirit, gently bringing forth God's justice to all the earth, not calling attention to himself but serenely accomplishing God's purpose: "a light for the nations, to open the eyes of the blind." "I am the light of the world," he will say, and by that light we will find our way back to the God who loves us and patiently waits for us to follow his Son home to him.

Death (but also its defeat) is in the air. Lazarus, whom Jesus had returned to life not long before, hosted the banquet. Martha, of course, cooked and served. Their sister Mary, who hung on every word of Jesus, took the opportunity as hostess to do him honor by personally making him welcome. The genuine (nice detail) aromatic nard which she used on Jesus was of the highest quality, as became evident to all as the house was filled with its fragrance. Jesus uses Judas' harrumphing about the waste of money to look into the future, when his body (put to death by Judas' betrayal!) will need anointing. The closing remarks show the chief priests' plot to kill Jesus extends even to Lazarus. It's getting scary....

Tuesday of Holy Week

Scripture

Isaiah 49: 1-6 *The Lord called me from birth, from my mother's womb he gave me my name. / You are my servant, he said to me, through whom I show my glory. / It is too little, he says, for you to be my servant, to raise up the tribes of Jacob and restore the survivors of Israel. / I will make you a light to the nations, that my salvation may reach to the ends of the earth.*

Responsorial Psalm 71: 1-2, 3-4, 5-6, 15, 17

John 13: 21-33, 36-38 *Jesus, reclining with his disciples, grew deeply troubled: "One of you will betray me." The disciples looked at one another, puzzled as to whom he could mean. "Lord, who is he?" "The one to whom I give the bit of food I dip in the dish." He gave it to Judas [and] Satan entered his heart. No sooner had Judas eaten the morsel than he went out. It was night. [And] Jesus said, "I am not to be with you much longer."*

Reflection:
The second song of the Suffering Servant describes the role Jesus is to play as our Messiah, and as the Savior of the world. Even this setback cannot stop him: "Though I thought I had toiled in vain, and uselessly spent my strength, / I am made glorious in the sight of the Lord, and my God is now my strength! / I will make you a light to the nations, [he says], that my salvation may reach to the ends of the earth." It may have seemed he was toiling uselessly and accomplishing nothing, but God has become his strength, and will use him to bring salvation not just to Jacob and Israel (the southern and northern kingdoms), but even to the Gentiles, to all the world! Now, there's a mission fit for a Messiah! Meanwhile, back at the ranch...our Lord is sadly acknowledging his coming betrayal—by one of his own, one of his handpicked twelve. Satan enters the heart of Judas, and all becomes dark: "it was night." A world away from the light that Jesus is bringing from the Father of Lights (James 1:17), from whom is every perfect gift from above. How awful it would be for us to reject the gift of Jesus, to turn off the light he has filled us with, to choose to return to the darkness of sin...and yet, it's because we keep doing it that Jesus becomes the Suffering and Saving Servant whom the Father sends so the whole world can be saved. What a sacrifice for Jesus...what a gain for us. Let's be grateful.

Wednesday of Holy Week

Scripture

Isaiah 50: 4-9 This selection appeared last Sunday as first reading for the Mass, p. 90.

Responsorial Psalm 69: 8-10, 21-22, 31. 33-34
(This could well be the Servant's Prayer) *For your sake I bear insult. I have become an outcast to my brothers, and the insults of those who blaspheme you fall upon me. Insult has broken my heart, and I am weak. I looked for sympathy, but there was none. Rather, in my thirst they gave me vinegar to drink. I will praise the name of God, and I will glorify him with thanksgiving, for the Lord hears the poor.*

Matthew 26: 14-25 *Judas Iscariot went to the chief priests and said, "What are you willing to give me if I hand [Jesus] over to you?" They paid him thirty pieces of silver, and from that time on he [looked] for an opportunity to hand him over. [When] the disciples prepared the Passover supper [Jesus] reclined at table with the Twelve [and] said "One of you is about to betray me." Judas, his betrayer, spoke: "Surely it is not I, Rabbi?" Jesus answered, "It is you who have said it."*

Reflection:

The faithful servant keeps at his task, but he is reviled and beaten instead of appreciated. "Insult has broken my heart, and shame covers my face." The vinegar-to-drink bit (verse 22) is almost certainly the source (quoted inexactly) for Matthew 27: 34 "they gave Jesus wine to drink mixed with gall" (see also Mark 15: 23 "wine drugged with myrrh," a narcotic). In the end, the Servant endures: "the Lord God is my help, I am not disgraced. He is near who upholds my right."

In the gospel, Jesus sends his disciples ahead to prepare, to tell the man, "The Teacher says, 'My appointed time draws near. I am to celebrate the

Passover with my disciples in your house.'" That "appointed time" drawing near has an ominous tone, since one of his own, his trusted ones, is about to betray him. "The Son of Man is departing, as Scriptures says of him, but woe to that man by whom [he] is betrayed."

Good old Jesus…this is not a threat he's calling down in wrath. It's a soulful sorrow that one of us could be so blind, so misguided, that for any amount of money (or pleasure, or whatever…you fill in the blank) we could toss aside his offer of redeeming love and ignore his Father's outstretched hand. How can we ever turn our backs on Jesus, knowing what it has cost him to make his Father's love so evident—and so close—to us?

Gentle reader:
This brings us to the end of Lent. I hope the journey has been fruitful. We've come to the threshold of the special season of the Holy Triduum (Holy Thursday, Good Friday, and Holy Saturday Night) our high holy days. May these celebrations make your faith come alive. Please consult Barren Earth To New Growth, another contribution by the same grateful author, which studies the Triduum and the feasts following Easter, and is available through this website or at religious shops/bookstores.
Thank you, and God bless you.